Jeniece & Rohan,

I'm so happy to share the Anger Myth with the two of you. I hope you will read a chapter a week together, discuss it, and enjoy the exercises as a couple.

Create all the room you need for more LOVE, MONEY, and PURPOSE in your lives!

Much Love,

Trish

3-15-25

The Anger Myth

The Anger Myth

Understanding and Overcoming the Mental Habits That Steal Your Joy

Trish Ahjel Roberts
Foreword by Jack Canfield

ROWMAN & LITTLEFIELD
Lanham • Boulder • New York • London

Published by Rowman & Littlefield
An imprint of The Rowman & Littlefield Publishing Group, Inc.
4501 Forbes Boulevard, Suite 200, Lanham, Maryland 20706
www.rowman.com

86-90 Paul Street, London EC2A 4NE

British Library Cataloguing in Publication Information Available

Library of Congress Cataloging-in-Publication Data

Names: Roberts, Trish Ahjel, author.
Title: The anger myth : understanding and overcoming the mental habits that steal your joy / Trish Ahjel Roberts ; foreword by Jack Canfield.
Description: Lanham : Rowman & Littlefield, [2024] | Includes bibliographical references and index.
Identifiers: LCCN 2023039102 (print) | LCCN 2023039103 (ebook) | ISBN 9781538180945 (cloth) | ISBN 9781538180945 (ebook)
Subjects: LCSH: Anger--Management.
Classification: LCC BF575.A5 R554 2024 (print) | LCC BF575.A5 (ebook) | DDC 152.4/7--dc23/eng/20231205
LC record available at https://lccn.loc.gov/2023039102
LC ebook record available at https://lccn.loc.gov/2023039103

Praise for *The Anger Myth*

"I met Trish Ahjel Roberts in 2021 when we worked together on her previous book, *12 Steps to Mind-Blowing Happiness*, and I'm so impressed with her work. Picking up where that book left off, *The Anger Myth* highlights the perils of anger and offers creative and powerful solutions. With compelling stories and deep wisdom, Trish presents life-changing lessons on managing negative emotions. Given all the fear and unhappiness in the world today, *The Anger Myth* should be on every bookshelf."

—**Marci Shimof**f, #1 *New York Times* bestselling author, *Happy for No Reason* and featured teacher in *The Secret*

"To Thích Nhất Hạnh's *Anger: Wisdom for Cooling the Flames*, we must add Trish Ahjel Roberts' *The Anger Myth* to the list of Buddhist-inspired books addressing this most destructive of human emotions. The title of Roberts's book reveals the first, most important truth about anger that most people not only don't understand, but misunderstand—anger is 100% destructive by nature; it has no redeeming qualities. After establishing that perspective, with the assistance of the Buddhist teacher we share, Geshe Kelsang Gyatso, Roberts launches into her five-step process for addressing and diminishing one's anger. For someone like myself, who constantly struggles with violent reactions to injustice, expanding one's toolkit for grappling with this ruinous mental action is a welcome balm in an oft-times ugly world."

—**Paul B. Chen**, Publisher, *Natural Awakenings Atlanta*

"I met Trish at a mastermind with my business partner in 2021. She stood out of the pack with her desire to help people grow and her passion for her work. *The Anger Myth* is a balm in a chaotic world. Trish teaches the reader how to transform negative emotions like anger, jealousy, and frustration into peace and positive action through her brand of mindset-shifting techniques. Everyone can benefit from reading *The Anger Myth* and incorporating the five-step Tame and Reframe method into their lives."

—**Patty Aubery**, #1 *New York Times* bestselling author of *Permission Granted* and Co-Creator of the *Chicken Soup for the Soul*® brand

"As a yoga and meditation practitioner, Ahimsa, or non-harming, is one of the core principles I share with my students. Through the lens of *The Anger Myth*, we become aware of the potential damage of uncontrolled anger—both within ourselves and the broader community. Trish weaves together teachings from yoga, Buddhism, and life coaching, distilling them into a concise five-step process that offers the potential to transmute negative emotions into profoundly positive actions. This is great book to add to your personal collection as you flow along a path toward wellness and spiritual growth."

—**Faith Hunter**, Author of *Spiritually Fly: Wisdom, Meditation and Yoga to Elevate Your Soul*

"Drawing from ancient Buddhist wisdom, Trish Ahjel Roberts offers a deep dive into understanding and overcoming anger in our daily life. With real-life, relatable examples, and thoughtful exercises, this guide helps readers pinpoint the destructive tendencies of anger in their own mind, and craft a step-by-step plan to uproot them. A timely book, given the destructive state of our world. World peace depends upon each individual eradicating the anger from within."

—**Mayra Cuevas**, Award-winning author and journalist

"I first reached out to Trish in 2022 to collaborate on the topic of trauma and how it impacts wellness. Since then, I've had the opportunity to work with her on a number of projects. She always brings a unique perspective and careful analysis to her work. *The Anger Myth* incorporates Trish's training in life coaching, Buddhism, and yoga along with in-depth research to offer a new approach to healing from negative emotions for both physical and mental health."

—**Serena Satcher**, MD, Integrative and Functional Medicine Physician, Roswell, GA

"*The Anger Myth* is a refreshing guide on how you can remove anger from your life. Trish discusses emotions not normally associated with anger in a new way. She introduces what she calls Anger's 7 Cranky Cousins: disappointment, annoyance, frustration, jealousy, impatience, guilt, and resentment. By providing helpful stories and MythBuster Exercises she teaches how to process negative emotions using meditation, journaling, breathwork, and imagination. Finally, she shows us the possibilities awaiting us in the space where anger used to be. We all just need a little courage to start the process. If you are looking to evolve to a happier and more peaceful life, *The Anger Myth* is for you!"

—**Natasha Brewley (Chef Beee)**, MBA, PhD, HHC, Owner of Essentially Chef Beee and Nyansapo Wellness Institute, Inc.

"I've known Trish for years as part of her Black Vegan Life® community. *The Anger Myth* teaches you how to develop empathy as part of her five-step Tame and Reframe method to alleviate anger and increase happiness. Trish goes even further by explaining the difference between sympathy, empathy, and compassion, so you can move from 'feeling bad' to 'doing good.' *The Anger Myth* will help you relieve the frustration, worry, and guilt that weigh you down while giving you ideas and education to lift you up, including information about a cruelty-free lifestyle."

—**Christopher "Soul" Eubanks**, Founder and CEO, Apex Advocacy, Atlanta, GA

"*The Anger Myth* is a transformative program that equips individuals with effective strategies to manage their emotional states and take control of their lives. Through the Tame and Reframe method, Trish breaks down a practical five-step approach to transforming negative emotions. With *The Anger Myth*, individuals can experience breakthroughs in their emotional and mental well-being, as they learn to overcome negative thought patterns and cultivate a more positive and empowered mindset."

—**Michelle Young**, C-IAYT Yoga Therapist, E-RYT 500, Founder of My Vinyasa Practice, Austin, TX

"I have known Trish since she first started her Black Vegan Life® group on Meetup back in 2014. She would bring a bunch of folks to my vegan cooking class in Atlanta just about every month. She always sat in the front and asked questions, clearly curious and wanting to learn. It's such a pleasure seeing her spread her wisdom in *The Anger Myth*. She has taken so many different wisdom philosophies to create her five-step Tame and Reframe technique to transform anger. She incorporates breathwork from yoga, philosophy from Buddhism, compassion from veganism, positive psychology, habit theory, and more. *The Anger Myth* is chock full of powerful information and techniques to make your life more peaceful and purposeful."

—**Neeta Sanders**, Co-Founder, Soul2Soul Educare, Atlanta, GA

"Trish's Yoga Nidra | Awak{end} Sleep™ certification is a testament to her dedication and passion for yoga. I had the pleasure of leading the training at an Ashram in Atlanta, and I am thrilled to see her sharing her talents with the world. Her book, *The Anger Myth* is a powerful tool that uses Buddhist philosophy and yoga teachings to help you become more mindful and transform negativity. It truly helps you to create a peaceful and purposeful life amidst the chaos of this world."

—**Chitra Sukhu**, Creator of Yoga Nidra | Awak{end}
Sleep™ System, Spiritual Teacher, and Mystic

Disclaimers

This book is not intended to be a substitute for mental or physical healthcare from a qualified provider.

The stories in this book are based on compilations of various sources and do not represent the experiences or opinions of any specific individuals.

*This book is dedicated to my daughter Kayla
and every person seeking Mind-Blowing Happiness.
Always know that you have the power to create the life you desire.
Joy happens from the inside out.*

Contents

Foreword

If you want more joy in your life, you are in the right place. I first met Trish Ahjel Roberts in the beginning of 2021 during a mastermind retreat I hosted with my longtime friends and business associates Steve Harrison and Patty Aubery. After one of the most disruptive and turbulent years in recent history, Trish was promoting her book *12 Steps to Mind-Blowing Happiness.* As part of the retreat, I interviewed Trish and asked her what the most important step was out of her twelve. Without hesitation, she said anger and all its related emotions—disappointment, annoyance, frustration, resentment, and more—keep good people from living the joyful lives they desire for themselves. She explained that people must learn to transform their anger into either calm or constructive action. Anger by itself isn't helpful at all, and it's impossible to make a good decision or experience happiness when you are angry. I couldn't agree more. If you've ever been really riled up, you know it's true.

The thing is, most people don't realize that they have another option. The mistaken idea that anger is useful or necessary is what Trish calls the Anger Myth. She provides all the evidence you need to make you a believer. She offers data, examples, stories, and the opportunity for you to reflect on the role anger and other negative emotions have played in your own life. You will realize that often when you think anger is motivating you, it is akin to using a sledgehammer to crack a walnut. You could do more with much less. And you pulled a muscle with the sledgehammer—you damaged yourself. When you wield anger, it does the same thing.

If you saw the film *The Secret*, you know that I am a big believer in the law of attraction, the idea that you have the power to attract into your life what you think about and desire most. In other words, thoughts become things. In the same way that positive thoughts become positive things, negative thoughts become negative things. *The Anger Myth* teaches you how to reclaim control of your thoughts through meditation, positive affirmations, breathwork, and a host of other techniques to manifest the life you want the most.

The Anger Myth couldn't have come at a better time. If you follow the news, you have seen the proliferation of anger, hatred, and violence around the world. It doesn't have to be this way. By learning and implementing time-tested techniques in *The Anger Myth*, you can become calmer, happier, more fulfilled, and more productive.

Trish is the perfect person to write this book. She has been studying Buddhist principles and yoga philosophy for more than ten years. She is a certified life coach, career coach, and teacher. She is trained as an energy healer and meditation instructor. And despite surviving all types of trauma in her life, she's one of the happiest people I know. I'm certain that if you follow the recommendations in her beautiful book, not only will you free yourself from anger, you will open up to a world of joy.

—**Jack Canfield**, coauthor of the #1 *New York Times* bestselling
Chicken Soup for the Soul® series and *The Success Principles*™:
How to Get from Where You Are to Where You Want to Be

Introduction

What Is the Anger Myth?

Are you tired of feeling angry? Perhaps you don't think of yourself as angry, just disappointed, annoyed, or frustrated with aspects of your life. You might find yourself experiencing jealousy, impatience, guilt, or resentment. In your hand is a simple book with the potential to change your life forever. This is an opportunity to live a more joyful life, achieve more of what's important to you, and improve your life permanently. Your decision to address anger in your life is a wise move that many people don't have the courage to make. Many years ago, I read *The Road Less Traveled* by M. Scott Peck. In it he said, "Evil people hate the light because it reveals themselves to themselves."[1] Those words stayed with me. It is difficult to acknowledge and address our negative qualities. However, if you want a deeply joyful, fulfilled, and satisfying life, you have to work on yourself. You cannot hide from yourself. You are the common denominator in every aspect of your life.

While anger is common, *The Anger Myth* will explain why anger is *never* productive and always relays false information. Simply put, anger lies. In this book, I will provide all the tools you need to remove anger from your life. Get ready for relatable and motivating stories on the perils of anger combined with real data on the costs to *you*. You will learn a new approach to remove anger from your life so you can spend more time enjoying yourself and doing things that are satisfying, fulfilling, and productive.

I didn't always know the lessons I teach here. I began to learn the truth about anger in 2010. I was a divorced single mom with a nine-year-old daughter living in a new city. I was in the midst of a painful breakup with my boyfriend, and every day when I went to work, I was convinced that my boss hated me. The job was hard, but the money was small. Bills were piling up, and I was exhausted. My confidence was taking a beating, and I found myself hiding under dull gray sweaters all the time. I had put so much time and effort into my education and my career, and nothing was working out. I was sad, disappointed, frustrated, overwhelmed, angry, and stuck. My parents tried to help, but I could see the dismay in their eyes. It broke my heart. I couldn't see a way out and wondered what I had done to deserve this.

One day after work, I sat at my kitchen table and googled the word "meditation." I had always been curious and hoped it might help. As soon as I clicked enter, a meditation center popped up not far from my office that offered a thirty-minute lunchtime session. It was perfect! I signed up.

The next day was all blue skies and sunny. I jumped into my little beige Beetle, fought Atlanta traffic, and finally pulled into the gravel driveway to what looked like a big country inn. A kind-looking man opened the door, pointed me to the living room, and told me to take off my shoes. I walked on the hardwood floor barefoot, glad I had just gotten my toes done. Then I saw big golden Buddha statues that almost reached the ceiling. In front of them were little crystal bowls of water, candies, and flowers. The sun came into the room through huge windows. I felt a sense of peace come over me. It was all so beautiful.

A middle-aged woman walked in looking like she'd just stepped out of a J. Crew catalog, with khaki pants and a pale pink top. She wrinkled her nose and said, "Well, since you're the only one here, maybe we can change the meditation I had planned for today. I don't know if you'll like it."

I didn't understand. *Why wouldn't I like the meditation?* I assured her that I was game for whatever meditation she had in mind.

She asked me if I wanted to sit in chairs or on the floor. I opted for the floor, so we sat on pillows on the hardwood floor. Then she dropped the bomb: "Today's meditation is about death," she said.

Death, of course, because my life is a disaster, I thought. I smiled at her and said, "That's perfect!" I didn't know anything about meditation, but somehow, I knew that focusing on death would help me appreciate my life.

She explained that while people intellectually know they will die someday, they go through life believing each day when they wake up that they still have time until the day arrives when they no longer have time, and they are surprised.

She gave me a mantra to say with her: "I could die today." We repeated it over and over. "I could die today. I could die today." We sat in silence. I felt a shift inside of me. It was like the scene at the end of *The Wizard of Oz* when Dorothy realizes all she had to do to return home was click her heels together three times and repeat, "There's no place like home. There's no place like home. There's no place like home." I realized I could access my internal, spiritual home any time I needed to.

After our session ended, I gave her a hug, and the warmth of her embrace startled me. I nearly skipped down the gravel road back to my car. My life was changed forever. It was like a near-death experience, but I felt like I had come alive. I became more curious. *What else don't I know?* I started taking classes every week, studying every day, and exploring more healing and wisdom traditions and modalities.

The woman in the pink top taught me that life is short and small hugs can make a big difference. We are still friends today. I am forever grateful for the moment that shift took place in my life. If you follow the lessons of *The Anger Myth*, this moment may be one you will always remember, the same way I remember sitting at my kitchen table and googling the word "meditation." So often we think our lives change in big moments, like new jobs, new babies, or graduations, but many times it's the tiny shifts that change our course. When you come to understand the Anger Myth for yourself, your life will never be the same. It will take you down a new path that you didn't know existed, on a road to freedom, joy, and authentic happiness.

After more than a decade of Buddhist study and yoga experience, I left my corporate job and launched my coaching business. I am a certified life coach, registered yoga and meditation instructor, and certified reiki practitioner. I authored the Amazon bestselling inspirational journal *12 Steps to Mind-Blowing Happiness: A Journal of Insights, Quotes & Questions to Juice Up Your Journey*, which has been endorsed by Jack Canfield, Marci Shimoff, and Iyanla Vanzant. I speak to people all over the world on the topics of anger, compassion, and happiness. And today, I'm here with you as your guide.

The Anger Myth begins with a quiz: "What's Your Anger Quotient?" This will provide your initial benchmark. From there, it is structured in three parts. Part 1, "The Myth," will show you how anger works to destroy your peace and why it is *never* helpful. Part 2, "The Five-Step Solution—Tame and Reframe" will teach you a new approach to transform anger in any situation to either peace or constructive action. Finally, Part 3, "The Side Effect," will introduce you to what seems impossible right now: the joy of a life free from anger. I encourage you to use a designated journal or notebook as you work through this book. If you prefer, you can take notes on a smartphone or other electronic device. At the end of each chapter, you will find key points and an Anger MythBuster exercise to help you **process** and **practice** what you have learned. After you finish the reading and exercises in all twelve chapters, take the quiz again so you can see your progress. If you read each chapter completely and do the Anger MythBuster exercises, you will be shocked by how much you will reduce and even completely alleviate your anger. The final chapter will teach you how to continue your progress by either working with someone else or learning to coach yourself.

You may be tempted to skip around in this book, but I encourage you to read straight through and complete the exercises at the end of each chapter in order. Some people like to skim through the entire book and then go back to work through the exercises. Feel free to take that approach as well. I have included subheadings to make *The Anger Myth* easy to skim, easy to read, and easy to use as a resource as often as needed.

There are moments in our lives that change us permanently—those *aha!* moments we all long for. Anger happens when we don't get our own way. *The Anger Myth* will teach you how to process your reaction when things don't happen the way you would like them to in a way that helps rather than harms you. I hope you are as excited to embark on this journey as I am to guide you. Now that you know what to expect, what are you waiting for? Let's get started on your first step toward living a life without anger on a path to what I call Mind-Blowing Happiness.

WHAT'S YOUR ANGER QUOTIENT?
TAKE THE QUIZ

Take the quiz below to learn your Anger Quotient. Use this information to follow your progress. Complete the prompts now, then take the quiz again after you finish working through this book. Take another assessment six months later as you incorporate what you've learned into your life. You can also take the quiz online at TheAngerMyth.com.

The Anger Myth Assessment
(Learn Your Anger Quotient)

Assign each statement a score of 1 to 5, with 1 being "never" and 5 being "always."

1. If someone bumps into you while walking, you get angry. ____
2. You hold on to grudges for a long time. ____
3. You like to get revenge when people offend or disrespect you. ____
4. If someone cuts you off in traffic, you immediately get angry. ____
5. You often get mad at yourself. ____
6. If the weather is bad when you have an event planned, you get upset. ____
7. You are angry with people who you have never told. ____
8. You feel jealous of other people. ____
9. You get impatient when you have to wait in line. ____
10. You often feel interrupted and dismissed in conversations. ____
11. You often yell at family and friends. ____
12. You often fight with people physically. ____

Total your answers: ____

Assessing Your Anger Quotient

48–60: Your relationship with anger needs some work. You are not alone. The good news is that *The Anger Myth* is the perfect place to learn to transform anger and create a more joyful life. If you find yourself feeling depressed or overwhelmed, seek counseling from a certified mental health professional. Feelings cannot destroy you. You can get control of anger and become happier. Stay the course.

36–47: You're in the middle of the pack, not quite sunshine and rainbows, but holding it all together. You've got lots of company. Keep doing the work and you will see progress. Life is about to get a whole lot better. Work through all the Anger MythBuster exercises, and **process** and **practice** each step. The best is yet to come!

24–35: Look at you smiling peacefully like you've got a secret! You are doing a great job transforming anger in your life and following the path of Mind-Blowing Happiness. Keep up the amazing work! You're heading toward the sweetest part of the journey! Continue to work through the Anger MythBuster exercises that resonate with you most and **process** and **practice** each step. You are a star!

12–23: Congratulations! If you are in this range, you have gotten so good at this anger thing, you have truly embraced the Anger Myth and hardly notice anger or its 7 Cranky Cousins in your life. You are now enjoying the side effect of authentic happiness. Don't stop your journey here. Continue to **process** and **practice** using the Tame and Reframe technique, and enjoy your joy and peace!

PART ONE

The Myth

Chapter 1

Why Anger Never Works

Anger is the result of things not going your way.

There is a lot of confusion about anger. Some people say it is necessary. Some believe it is a motivator. One thing we can all agree on is that it does not feel good to hold on to anger. Even a brief flash of anger can be painful. You may have been taught to "release" your anger by hitting an object, throwing something, yelling, bullying, or fighting. However, at the end of this "release" you will find that the anger easily reemerges, perhaps in a different form than before. It may look like disappointment, annoyance, frustration, jealousy, impatience, guilt, resentment, self-loathing, depression, hatred, or any type of ongoing turbulence in the undercurrent of your life.

The Anger Myth is for people who want to be free from anger in all its forms, whether it is subtle frustration, full-blown rage, or anything in between.

**Every form of anger is destructive. Always. Period.
Anger always lies.**

By learning to transform and extinguish your anger permanently, you will open the door to a life that is both peaceful and what I call "juicy." A juicy life is rich and satisfying, much like your favorite summer fruit, a home-cooked meal, or a decadent dessert. It is a life aligned with truth rather than the misinformation triggered by anger.

Anger can be defined as "a strong feeling of displeasure and usually of antagonism"[1] or even, "the strong emotion that you feel when you think someone has behaved in an unfair, cruel, or unacceptable

3

way."[2] These simple definitions describe the feeling of anger but do not deal with the results. Anger always has results, and they are never good. In his book *How to Solve Our Human Problems*, Geshe Kelsang Gyatso says, "Anger is a deluded mind that focuses on an animate or inanimate object, feels it to be unattractive, exaggerates its bad qualities, and wishes to harm it."[3]

Anger has intent. Its intent is to do harm. When it does not harm others, it harms itself. Anger always exaggerates. Exaggerations are lies. Anger lies. Every. Single. Time.

THE 8-PAT: EIGHT PRIMARY ANGER TRIGGERS

There are many factors that can cause anger. The Eight Primary Anger Triggers (also known as the 8-PAT) are some of the biggest. I'm sure you will find many, if not all, of them to be all too familiar. As you work through this text, we will revisit the 8-PAT often.

1. **Relationships:** Whether they are with romantic partners, family, friends, coworkers, or those in your community, your relationships have a major impact on your life. Their importance and complexity can create both joy and friction.
2. **Driving:** Your experience operating motorized vehicles creates a unique opportunity for tension. Partial anonymity, heightened potential for injury, legal regulations, and rushing to important events can create a stressful environment.
3. **Society:** The world is a big, complex place so there are many issues that can cause anger, whether it's discrimination, injustice, environmental issues, or any of a host of societal problems.
4. **Politics:** From the Roman Empire to modern democracies, issues around government have long been a cause for contention. Whether it's laws, regulations, taxes, or representation, there is plenty of opportunity for discontent.
5. **Losses:** You have probably experienced many losses in your life. Loss is a natural part of life that cannot be avoided. Whether you lose a loved one, a job, your health, or your youth, any loss is difficult and can lead to anger.

6. **Choices:** You make many choices throughout your life: big choices like your education or occupation and small choices like where to go for dinner or vacation. You might change jobs or change partners. And at times you may regret your decisions and find yourself grappling with anger.
7. **Life in General:** You might feel that you got the short end of the stick in life overall. Maybe you didn't get a good start with your family, your neighborhood, or the opportunities available to you. You might feel cheated and upset.
8. **Self:** If you've ever missed a goal, lost a promotion, or failed to keep a promise, you may have found yourself angry with *yourself*. You might have questioned your effort, commitment, or follow-through and gotten stuck in self-directed anger.

The following stories based on real-life situations will give you the opportunity to explore your anger triggers and begin to find solutions.

I. Relationships

Your connections with your friends, family, and partners can be a source of great joy. The people closest to you are also a major source of anger simply because of their proximity. These are the people with whom you have the most contact. When you are unhappy about anything, these are also the people who feel the most fallout.

- *Romantic Partners*
  It's normal to have occasional disagreements with your romantic partner. After all, you might share your home and possessions with your partner, along with your deepest feelings.
  Tina J. was addressing an issue with her husband. He made an offhand remark that hurt her feelings. She got angry. In a flash, she forgot all his good qualities and was intent on harming him. She said something to cut him deep. He walked out the door. After having some time to think, Tina realized her husband's remark was not meant to hurt her and that she had misunderstood him. Later that evening, Tina apologized. She said she didn't know what came over her. She had gotten angry. Now she had to deal with the issue that caused the original argument *and* repair the relationship from

the damage done by the hateful words she said to the husband she loves. She started with one problem and ended up with three: the original issue, the damage she caused, and the damage her husband may have caused from acting on his anger. If this pattern repeats, over time it will destroy their relationship. Even if they manage to stay together, the level of happiness in their relationship will gradually decline unless they learn how to manage disagreements without resorting to anger.

Why is this anger a lie?
Tina could no longer see the good qualities in her partner and wanted to harm him as if he were not a person she loved. Anger was the lie that made him invisible.

- *Parents*
  Just about everyone has issues with their parents. It is the nature of the generational divide. You might even feel like your parents were particularly lacking. Perhaps they sent you to live with someone else and you felt abandoned as a child. Maybe your parents were unavailable because of addictions, mental illness, physical ailments, immigration status, or incarceration. You might have had parents who were present in your life but made you feel unsupported or unloved because of verbal, physical, sexual, or emotional abuse; teasing; or sibling favoritism. Perhaps your parents thought children should be "seen and not heard" and didn't acknowledge your emotions or contribution to the family. Any of these issues can create trauma and a need for healing. They can also manifest as deeply rooted anger.

  Paul S. was frequently told to get a switch or branch from a tree and bring it to his father for a beating. As he got older, his anger toward his father grew. He wanted his father's love and affection; instead, he was ashamed and embarrassed by his father's use of physical and emotional violence as punishment. (Sending a person to select the weapon that will be used against them is most certainly emotional violence.) When his father wasn't "disciplining" him, it seemed they had no relationship. His father paid more attention to other people than to his first-born son. Paul's anger made him feel strong in the face of the deep pain he felt from parental abuse and neglect. It made him want to lash out. It also gave him headaches and damaged his relationship with his wife and his father-in-law.

Why is this anger a lie?
Paul was traumatized as a child
and held on to deeply rooted pain.
Anger was the lie that covered up his feelings
of violation and abandonment.

- *Siblings*

Siblings fight for all kinds of reasons, many of them stemming from family dynamics in childhood. There may have been a parental preference for the first-born, the youngest, or the child who was deemed prettier, smarter, or more popular in school. There may have been struggles over resources like the best food, clothing, toys, or sleeping arrangements. There may have been siblings with disabilities like genetic disease, dyslexia, autism, mental illness, juvenile diabetes, or cancer. There may have been siblings who experienced trauma as a result of bullying, assault, or sexual violence. There is no limit to the possibilities for comparison and contention.

Katrina N. was the oldest of five siblings. She felt she got the brunt of the discipline and that her parents were easier on her younger siblings. She also had to take on the bulk of the responsibility. She had to take care of her younger siblings while her parents worked. She felt intense pressure to do well in school to "set an example" for the other kids. Many times, she would pick up behind her siblings only to have them make a mess again. Her parents told her she was responsible because she was the oldest. Over the years, she developed a lot of resentment toward her younger siblings, especially the baby. The baby had no responsibility at all! It was a complete insult.

Katrina never acknowledged any outward anger toward her siblings, but she was on a slow simmer. She would complain that her brothers and sisters were lazy, didn't have any responsibility, and didn't appreciate her. But if you asked the younger siblings, they would tell you Katrina got the best of everything: the newest clothes, the best bedroom, and the opportunity to indulge herself with dance and music lessons. They thought Katrina was overbearing and was favored by her parents. While Katrina felt pressure to be a perfect "lieutenant parent," her siblings were feeling overlooked and jealous. Katrina's anger didn't allow her to see her siblings' side of things. It wasn't until she acknowledged their pain as well as her own that they were able to move past sibling anger, jealousy, and rivalry and begin a path toward healing.

Why is this anger a lie?
First, Katrina saw only her side of the situation.
A partial view is a lie.
Second, she suffered under the weight of excessive responsibility because of her role in the family.
Anger was the lie that covered up her pain.

- *Children*

    The relationship between parent and child is uniquely rewarding and challenging. Parents have societal and legal responsibility for their children that they do not have in any other type of relationship. Children are often considered a reflection of one's parenting skills and can impact a family's standing in their community. A successful, well-adjusted child can be a source of pride for a family, while a child who struggles with low grades, unemployment, drug addiction, or incarceration can be a source of shame and disillusionment.

    Sonya G. had three teenagers who wore on her nerves with their various moods, complaints, and opinions. The youngest gave her the most trouble; she started having sex, experimenting with drugs, and sneaking around with an undesirable group of kids. Finally, Sonya got the worst call she could imagine: Her daughter had been arrested for shoplifting. Sonya was an exhausted single parent, already angry with the kids for not pulling their weight in the house. She was embarrassed that her daughter would steal from a neighborhood store. Now everyone in her community would know she was a terrible parent. When she picked her daughter up from the police station, she took her home and screamed at her so loud and so long she lost her voice. Sometimes she just wanted to run away, but she had three more years before the kids would all be grown.

> *Why is this anger a lie?*
> *Sonya was overwhelmed and exhausted and*
> *needed parenting support and resources.*
> *Yelling and losing control only worsen the situation.*
> *Anger was the lie that hid her emotional*
> *exhaustion and embarrassment.*

- *Friends*

   Many times, friends and acquaintances—whether from elementary school, college, work, sports, or other settings—can become sparring partners. Resentment can develop in any relationship. In long friendships, people grow and change over time; sometimes they grow apart.

   Tiffany R. had been friends with Abby since elementary school. Abby was a bridesmaid in her wedding. When Tiffany found out that Abby was having an affair with her husband, she wanted to kill her. Deep betrayal can knock the wind right out of your sails. Thankfully, Tiffany was able to work through her pain and grief with a qualified counselor. She may never understand the selfishness that motivated Abby or her now ex-husband. However, she does understand that when people are that cutthroat and devoid of values, they are best left to each other. Abby did Tiffany a favor by showing her own ruthless nature and her husband's lack of loyalty before she devoted any more time to those relationships. Thankfully, Tiffany did not act out violently against her husband or her "friend." You have probably heard of stories like this that end in murder and jail time. Thankfully, Tiffany did not let her anger rule her.

> *Why is this anger a lie?*
> *Tiffany was betrayed by her husband and her*
> *friend in the most profound way.*
> *She was in excruciating emotional pain.*
> *Anger was the lie that sought to alleviate this*
> *pain with thoughts of violence.*

- *Authority Figures*

   Managers and supervisors are authority figures, as are police officers, school administrators, and other officials. You probably enjoy the moments in your life when you feel free. Perhaps you can decide what you want for dinner, which road you will travel to work, or how you will spend your leisure time. Authority figures by their very nature have the power to take options away from you and issue penalties. Your boss might assign you to a project you don't like or require you to work overtime. If you don't, you might miss out on a promotion or even lose your job. Police officers might give you a ticket for an infraction like jaywalking, noise, or improper parking, or they can order you to move your vehicle or disperse a crowd. School administrators may impact your grades and your ability to qualify for federal grants, tuition reimbursement, and other benefits. If you work for someone else, you probably have frequent interaction with your manager, which makes it easier to lose your cool when you feel they are pushing your buttons.

Melody H. was sick and tired of her boss. She worked twelve-hour days with barely a thank-you. She had not received a raise in years. If she made a mistake, her manager would scream at her, sometimes in front of her peers. There were times when she locked herself in the bathroom and cried. Her face would get red and hot with her tears. She wanted to curse her boss out and quit, but she needed her job. Her exhaustion and humiliation boiled over into rage. But when she recognized just how terrified her boss was of her own supervisor, she began to have a bit of perspective. Melody was able to recognize the strain on her mental health and changed jobs without harboring anger toward her old boss.

Why is this anger a lie?
Melody was feeling humiliated, unappreciated and exhausted.
She saw her boss simply as an abuser until she realized that
her boss was part of a chain of abuse at the organization.
Anger was the lie that sought to convert her pain into rage.

II. Driving

When you get in your car, you face a whole host of potential stressors. There is a heightened possibility of physical harm to yourself, your passengers, and pedestrians that does not exist when you are on foot. You may be rushing to work, a job interview, or another important event that increases your stress levels. You typically cannot see the faces of the people passing the way you can when you are walking. As a driver, your actions are also highly regulated by law. If you feel oppressed, operating a motorized vehicle may give you a feeling of power that is not otherwise accessible in your daily life. This sense of anonymity, heightened stress, power, regulation, and potential for physical harm all create an environment conducive to anger.

Sheila B. was stuck in traffic on her way to work just about every day. She grumbled under her breath, honked her horn, and complained when she arrived at work almost daily. One day a driver cut her off and she accidentally ran into the back of his car. When the police arrived at the scene, she explained that it was not her fault, but she still received a ticket for following too closely. Sheila was livid. She cursed at the officers and threw a bottle at the other driver's car. The police arrested her for attempted assault, damaging property, and creating a disturbance. When she calmed down, she realized she had completely lost it. She now had an arrest record, her job was at risk, and she was humiliated and embarrassed by her own behavior.

Why is this anger a lie?
Sheila only focused on her perspective, never realizing
that all drivers were dealing with the same issues.
Because she didn't have a healthy way to manage the daily
stress of driving, she exploded when she got into an accident.
Anger was the lie that convinced her she had no responsibility
for the accident, when it had been brewing for months.

III. Society

There are many large societal issues that may cause anger. You may find yourself getting angry about injustice, environmental destruction, capitalism, racism, sexism, homophobia, transphobia, nationalism, xenophobia, animal abuse, or any other noble cause.

Amanda K. was eating dinner with her family the first time she saw the video of the murder of George Floyd. Her stomach lurched and she lost her appetite. As she tried to choke back tears, she felt a fiery rage rise from her belly. She cursed at the TV and yelled at her small children when they asked what was wrong. She got into a screaming match with her husband when he tried to calm her. The next morning, she woke up embarrassed that she had cursed in front of her kids. She had been so lost in her rage, she couldn't remember why she was arguing with her husband. The memory of the video made her nauseous again. Witnessing the killing of another unarmed Black man made her feel humiliated and betrayed, powerless to protect her sons. She felt herself sliding into anxiety and depression.

> *Why is this anger a lie?*
> *Amanda's outrage about the injustice she witnessed*
> *triggered deeply rooted pain for her.*
> *Instead of allowing herself to cry, which made her*
> *feel weak and vulnerable, she exploded in anger that*
> *harmed her family and that she later regretted.*
> *Anger was the lie that convinced her it could*
> *serve her better than her tears.*

IV. Politics

In the United States and across the world, politics has increasingly become a source of anger and contention. The relationship between government and citizen is often intense. People rely heavily on their governments for social order, while governments wield broad powers over commerce and the livelihood of their citizens. Meanwhile, politicians often flip-flop on critical issues to follow popular trends, withhold details about issues, and even lie outright to protect their political viability. Citizens may become so upset that they forget the benefits of government like social order, infrastructure like highways and bridges, military protection, income in retirement, unemployment assistance, and laws that provide for commerce and offer protection against violence and theft.

Shanna X. works long hours in a high-stress corporate job. She voted for a political candidate she believed would provide economic growth, access to healthcare, and more diversity in government. When multiple women came forth accusing the candidate of sexual assault, at first, she did not believe the women. However, once the trial began, it became obvious to her that the accusations were true. She felt like a fool. *How could she have been so stupid?* Shanna felt conned and humiliated by the candidate and betrayed by the entire political system that had covered up his bad behavior for so long. Even though she did careful research before voting, she began to doubt her own intelligence and competence. When friends and family wanted to discuss politics, she would get angry and say it didn't matter who you voted for—they're all disgusting idiots.

Why is this anger a lie?
Shanna's anger led her to falsely determine that all
political candidates are disgusting idiots.
Instead of managing feelings of betrayal, she doubted
herself and removed herself from the political process.
Anger was the lie that convinced her to throw in the towel.

V. Losses

Any loss is difficult. You can experience the loss of health, youth, privilege, or power. You might lose your job, home, or relationship. You may lose loved ones to death, either anticipated or unforeseen. In her 1969 book *On Death and Dying*, psychiatrist Elisabeth Kubler-Ross described the five stages of grief: denial, anger, bargaining, depression, and acceptance. Since then, her theory has become widely accepted, whether for the death of a person or any other loss.

Kevin F. worked at the same manufacturing company for twenty-five years. He was only six months away from qualifying for his full retirement package when his manager called him into his office. He thought he was being called to discuss retirement; instead, his manager fired him, citing "performance issues" that Kevin was not aware of. After the initial confusion and shock, Kevin erupted in rage. He told his boss exactly where he could shove his job, slamming the door on his way out. When he got into his car to drive home, he accidentally hit a curb and caused $500 in damage to his vehicle. After he left, he realized he didn't know if he was going to receive any severance pay or any other benefits. He had gotten so angry, he wasn't sure what his manager had said to him.

Why is this anger a lie?
Kevin was devastated by the magnitude of his loss and
embarrassed at having been caught so unprepared.
Anger was the lie that hid his pain and clouded
his ability to process information.

VI. Choices

Your life consists not only of the experiences you have but also of the choices you make. Everyone makes mistakes, and sometimes you may later regret your choices. These could be the choice of a partner, the decision to have (or not have) children, or the decision to pursue (or not pursue) a particular education or career. They could also include the neighborhood you choose to live in or the amount of debt you have accrued.

Sarah O. married at eighteen and was a mother of three by the time she was twenty-one. She loved her kids but found herself feeling resentful when some of her friends went off to college and started traveling overseas. Her husband was the only boyfriend she ever had, and she found herself jealous when her friends talked about dating and sex. She never had extra money to spend on herself, and she was tired most of the time. She worked all day as a hostess in a restaurant, and by the time she picked up the kids, helped them with homework, and gave them dinner, she was completely exhausted. She didn't think her husband helped enough with the kids, but she was tired of fighting about it. Her feelings of jealousy and resentment were always with her, often making her cranky and short-tempered with her family. She often found herself daydreaming of the life she might have had if she had waited to start a family.

Why is this anger a lie?
Sarah's jealousy told her the false narrative that
her friends have better lives than she does.
A loving family is something many people never
obtain, and continuing to follow this line of thinking
could very well cost Sarah her family.
Anger was the lie that made her focus on the negative aspects of
family life, ignore the benefits, and give up on making improvements.

VII. Life in General

Another common source of anger is a general dissatisfaction with life. Perhaps you thought you would have a better job, more disposable income, a better relationship, smarter children, or more money at a particular stage in your life. You may feel like you didn't have a good childhood, or perhaps you come from a hometown so small it makes you feel unimportant or so big it makes you feel invisible. Sometimes, even if you *have* the job, house, family, and money you hoped for, you still feel like something is missing. You might feel disconnected from family, community, or spirituality.

Derek N. entered the foster care system when he was only eight years old. He lived in twenty different homes and was bullied in school until he learned to fight. He spent most of his high school days fighting. By the time he was twenty, he was finishing up a prison sentence for his part in a petty crime. Life had been unfair, and he was angry. Other kids had parents who loved them and nice homes like he saw on TV. He got nothing but hard knocks over and over again. There was no point in trying. Things would never change.

Why is this anger a lie?
Derek was mad at the world because of his difficult experiences.
Anger was the lie that made him think things could never change.

VIII. Self

Sometimes you may find you are angry with yourself. Perhaps you set a goal and didn't achieve it, made a commitment to change your behavior and stumbled, started a business or project and failed, or made a promise and didn't keep it.

After the birth of her second child, Malina Y. couldn't get back into her work wardrobe. She bought new clothes to return to the office but was mad at herself for wasting her money. She tried to eat less, but the stress from being a full-time mother, wife, and employee made it difficult to find time to cook healthy meals or exercise. She told herself she was fat and that her husband would leave her if she didn't get it together. Her lack of confidence made her more withdrawn at home and work. One day her husband pinched her belly and smiled. She snapped at him, and he retreated. Malina had grown to hate her own body. Although she was a wonderful wife, mother, and employee, she couldn't see herself. After a few years, she finally found a program that worked for her and lost the weight. She was surprised to find that her relationships at home and work didn't change, and she was still upset about minor "flaws" in her body. Over the years, her husband noticed the drop in Malina's confidence and affection. He tried to compliment her no matter what size she was, but she couldn't seem to hear him. Two years after losing the weight, Malina was diagnosed with breast cancer. Now she longed for the chubby but healthy body that she took for granted.

Why is this anger a lie?
Malina was angry at her body and her ability to control it.
Anger was the lie is that made her see only the flaws in her
body and none of its healthfulness, functionality, and beauty.

KEY POINTS

1. Every form of anger is destructive. Always. Period. Anger relays false information. It always lies.
2. Anger can manifest in many different forms, including hatred, disappointment, frustration, annoyance, resentment, self-loathing, jealousy, depression, or any type of ongoing turbulence in the undercurrent of your life.
3. The Eight Primary Anger Triggers (8-PAT) are relationships, driving, society, politics, losses, choices, life in general, and self.
4. Anger *never* exists alone. It is *always* a cover for another emotion.
5. The appearance of anger *never* improves a situation.

There are many legitimate causes that spark intense emotion. However, anger always leads us in the wrong direction. Find a quiet space to spend thirty minutes or so working through the material below.

ANGER MYTHBUSTER EXERCISE

Process

1. Find a comfortable location in your home or other space. Take a few deep breaths, inhaling through your nose and exhaling through your mouth.
2. If you haven't already, take the Anger Myth Assessment at the beginning of this book.
3. Write your answers to the following questions in a notebook, journal, or electronic device:

- Which examples resonated the most with you?
- What situations did they remind you of in your own life?
- How did those situations play out?
- Describe the last time you got angry with someone else, a situation and yourself. Give one example of each, for a total of three examples. For each one, explain the results of your anger and identify the underlying emotion(s).

Practice

- Notice the next time you feel angry. When your anger subsides, reflect on any underlying emotions. Write them down.

Chapter 2

How Anger's 7 Cranky Cousins Steal Your Time, Money, Creativity, and Joy

Anger is sneaky.

Although anger comes in many forms, it always arises when things don't happen the way you want them to. Think about the last time you were angry. Maybe someone was rude to you, maybe you witnessed an injustice, or maybe someone stole from or lied to you. Perhaps you were expecting a package that never arrived or hoping for an outcome that didn't come to pass. You may have encountered one of Anger's 7 Cranky Cousins: disappointment, annoyance, frustration, jealousy, impatience, guilt, and resentment. While they may seem very different from what you usually think of as anger, they are all variations of the same underlying emotion—and each one will steal from you if you allow them to. In this way, anger is sneaky. It will show up and sit on your doorstep disguised as something else.

I first encountered this teaching in my Buddhist studies more than a decade ago, and it stopped me in my tracks. *Is anger really that deceptive?* Yes, it is, and I'll tell you why. Let's first look at the cranky cousins in a bit more detail.

ANGER'S 7 CRANKY COUSINS

Disappointment—Anger about a Perceived Loss

When you are disappointed, you experience a feeling of loss. You might have applied for a new job or a promotion. You might have asked someone out on a date. Maybe you failed an exam. Disappointment can be defined as "to fail to satisfy the hope, desire, or expectation of."[1] Everyone has experienced not getting what they want. How do you respond? Do you hang your head, complain to your friends, or yell about it? Does it take you hours, days, or even months to move on? While disappointment may seem like sadness, in reality it is one of the first levels of anger.

Annoyance—Anger about an Irritation, Often Repetitive

If you're like most people, you're familiar with the subtle rumbling of annoyance. The object of your ire is usually a repeat offender. Maybe a mosquito buzzed in your ear, your toddler called your name for the fiftieth time, or your partner left the refrigerator door open for the third time this week. To annoy is "to cause irritation to (another); make somewhat angry."[2] Like all of the 7 Cranky Cousins, if left unchecked, annoyance will keep you in a state of misery.

Frustration—Anger about Unresolved Issues

Have you ever tried to do something and repeatedly failed? Maybe you were putting together a piece of furniture, trying to bake a cake, or learning to roller skate. If so, you know how it feels to be frustrated. Frustration is "a deep chronic sense or state of insecurity and dissatisfaction arising from unresolved problems or unfulfilled needs."[3] Frustration can be the result of anything from trying to learn to knit to overall dissatisfaction with life. No matter the angle, its root is the same as all anger—things haven't gone as you planned.

Jealousy—Anger about Someone Else's Good Fortune

Shakespeare famously referenced the "green-eyed monster" in his work *Othello*. Feelings of jealousy are as old as Cain and Abel, and just as destructive. Leaning into jealousy doesn't work well, yet the advent of social media in the past few decades has arguably increased the desire to "keep up with the Joneses," competing with peers and neighbors for the best cars, homes, and lifestyle. This competition is a zero-sum game that cannot be won. Even the richest people on the planet cannot win the game of jealousy. There will always be someone with better health, more assets, better relationships, or smarter kids. Jealous can be defined as "hostile toward a rival or one believed to enjoy an advantage."[4] This hostility is a form of anger and serves no useful purpose.

Impatience—Anger about Having to Wait

In the course of everyday life, there are innumerable times when you have to wait, often at inconvenient times. You might be rushing to a business appointment, running late for a movie, or waiting in line to use the copy machine at the library. Maybe your flight was canceled, you were stuck in traffic, or you were last in line at the wedding buffet. Major life events can create more angst. Are you overdue to get married, buy a house, get a promotion, or have a baby? In her book *Super Attractor*, *New York Times* bestselling author and international speaker Gabby Bernstein describes her impatience waiting to get pregnant with her first child. Ultimately, she was able to lean into a sense of patience, which served her well. She shared, "My faith also gave me patience to trust that the Universe has a better plan than mine."[5]

Waiting is par for the course, but impatience can be avoided. Impatient can be defined as "restless or short of temper especially under irritation, delay, or opposition."[6] See the pattern? It's just another thinly veiled form of anger.

Guilt—Anger at Yourself

Most forms of anger are directed at others; guilt is different because its focus is inward. Guilt can be defined as "feelings of deserving blame especially for imagined offenses or from a sense of inadequacy."[7] This is not to be confused with guilt you *should* feel if you rob a bank, assault someone, or commit some other type of crime. This is guilt for imagined offenses like finishing a project late, appropriately disciplining your children, or deciding to stay home instead of attending a social event. You may have chosen not to cook the Christmas stuffing because you simply didn't have the time, then found yourself crushed with guilt over your decision. Guilt is an irrational form of anger focused on your own perceived shortcomings.

Resentment—Anger Extended over a Long Time

When feelings of subtle anger simmer for some time, they grow into resentment. Because it requires time, this feeling often develops in long-term relationships. Resentment can be defined as "a feeling of indignant displeasure or persistent ill will at something regarded as a wrong, insult, or injury."[8] Resentment is often tied to the other Cranky Cousins. For example, you may have grown up in a family where your brother was favored by your parents, resulting in feelings of jealousy. Spread over the decades of your lifetime, that jealousy can turn into a deep feeling of resentment.

Long-term romantic relationships are another perfect breeding ground for resentment. If your partner was unfaithful, you were probably sad, hurt, and disappointed. When you got together, you had an expectation of fidelity, and the betrayal represents a deep loss. Partners in many relationships go through the long, hard work to recover from this type of injury, and many are successful. However, the reverse is also true. Many marriages ultimately collapse under the weight of persistent feelings of disappointment, frustration, and jealousy. In other words, the betrayal becomes a resentment that is never resolved, and the relationship disintegrates.

* * *

Now that you've met Anger's 7 Cranky Cousins, let's look at how they impact your life.

WHAT THE 7 CRANKY COUSINS
STEAL FROM YOU

Time

While feelings of anger are common, as addressed in Chapter 1, they don't actually resolve issues. Small doses of time spent dissecting disagreements, imagining if things were different, and venting with friends, family, and anyone who will listen may serve to help you process your feelings. However, left unchecked, these activities do no more than take up your time. They can take on a life of their own and graduate to a questionable form of entertainment. We've all heard of—or known—people who enjoy creating drama in their lives. They've grown addicted to the adrenaline high of fussing, complaining, gossiping, yelling, and fighting. You may have even experienced this yourself. At the end of a disappointment binge or frustration campaign, you are left with nothing more than when you started. You may have processed some emotions, but often you end up feeling exhausted, bitter, confused, and powerless. Some people spend weeks, months, and even years overcome with their negative emotions, cycling through their guilt and resentment over and over, often finding themselves in a therapist's office in search of a pharmaceutical solution.

If you don't have a serious mental health diagnosis, you can learn to redirect your thoughts and regain control. If you do struggle with mental health issues, you may need medical support, but these techniques can give you more control.

Imagine what you could do if you had an extra hour every week. *What would you do with that time?*

Money

Some people say time is money, and for good reason. Time is one resource that cannot be replicated. Once an hour passes in the day, there is no way to get it back. So if you use your time following breadcrumbs into the swirling cesspool of Cranky Cousins, you will undoubtedly waste time. But will you really waste money? In movies like *The Wolf of Wall Street* and *Boiler Room*, short tempers and verbal abuse seem to be the key to wealth. The political landscape in Europe and the United States seems to show similar indications. So perhaps money follows greed (close kin to jealousy). If you believe that, you are partly right. People who want money but have no concern for integrity, relationships, or how their activities impact society can steal, lie, and cheat to obtain wealth, and often quite successfully. You, my dear reader, are not part of that pack. You want to improve yourself; that's why you're here.

For people who want to improve themselves, their families, and their communities by generating wealth, anger and its Cranky Cousins are a big waste of time. Disappointment, annoyance, and frustration slow you down. The faster you can transition away from them, then the faster you can move toward your goals and desires. Jealousy and impatience create an energetic debt. When you are jealous of someone else's success instead of being a cheerleader, you create an energy that inspires others to be jealous of you when you do well. Likewise, if you are impatient when you have to wait, you create an energy that inspires people to be impatient with you when you cause a delay.

Creativity

The Cranky Cousins steal your creativity by first stealing your time. When your energy is focused on complaining, there is little room for reflection, dreams for your future, or creative endeavors. To create is "to bring into existence" or "to produce through imaginative skill."[9] You may associate creativity with artists, dancers, or designers; but creativity is the realm of every person and is an essential component of joy. For most people, having an awareness of their talents and the ability to act upon them is deeply satisfying. This act of creation is the single most godlike experience most people will ever have. If you haven't experienced this in your own life, take a quick survey of people you know. Ask them, how does it feel when the task of creation is completed? Whether the creation is something temporary—like a sandcastle or a new hairstyle—or something more permanent—like a piece of furniture or a quilt—most people will report feeling genuine satisfaction.

But who has time to build a treehouse, write a song, start a business, or knit a sweater when they're constantly managing negative emotions? Angry art or melancholy musings might work to process difficult emotions, but there is a better way. Quickly learning to metabolize your anger in all its subtle forms frees up both the time and mental space necessary for creation.

Joy

The Cranky Cousins don't make us feel good. Not even when we call our friends and talk for hours about our problems. They can keep us up at night and be the first thing on our mind in the morning. It is impossible to experience disappointment, annoyance, frustration, jealousy, impatience, guilt, or resentment on a consistent basis and still have a sense of joy, happiness, and well-being. Ridding yourself of anger in all its forms is one of the best gifts you can give to yourself to improve the quality of your life. Anger and its Cranky Cousins are negative emotions that oppose the positive emotions we want to experience, like confidence, focus, wellness, and peacefulness.

* * *

Let's explore how the 7 Cranky Cousins impact our Eight Primary Anger Triggers (8-PAT) and steal our most precious resources: time, money, creativity, and joy.

I. Relationships

• *Romantic Partners*

Kaya J. was disappointed when her husband didn't get a hoped-for promotion. She tried to be encouraging when he gave her the news, but her body language told another story. Her eyes dropped and her shoulders slumped. She wanted the extra money for their family. It wasn't what she wanted or expected. She felt like he let her down.

It is normal to feel sad about a loss. However, Kaya's disappointment attached to her sadness and became a negative emotion directed at her husband. As with any form of anger, it is important to move through it as quickly as possible; otherwise, you risk wasting your time and losing the opportunity to experience more joy in your life. In Kaya's case, a long delay could also impact the family financially. Kaya's best route would be to support and encourage her husband so he can recover from the loss and move on to the next job interview or financial opportunity.

Another common example you may have seen or experienced is when one spouse or partner drinks too much at a party, making the other annoyed. Instead of waiting until the next day, they start an argument while one partner is still drunk. There's no better way to waste time than trying to argue with someone who is intoxicated. There are limitless examples of the possibilities for conflict in relationships. Learning to remove anger from disagreements will help you reclaim your time.

• *Parents*

Carole M.'s parents have been in a terrible, abusive relationship her whole life. She begged her mother to leave her father, but she refused. Even though her mom had a secure job working for the city government and could support herself financially, she said she made a vow to God that she could not break. Carole was frustrated. Every time Carole saw her mother, she pleaded with her to leave the relationship. They spent their time together arguing, spending less and less time together and eventually not speaking at all. Several years later, Carole's father called one day to let her know her mom had been diagnosed with cancer. Carole immediately drove to the hospital where her mother was receiving treatment. She started spending more time with her mother as her health continued to deteriorate. Of course, Carole had already lost the opportunity to spend time with a healthy mom. She regretted all the time she lost because she was frustrated with her mother's decision. Her mother died two years later. The lost time could never be regained.

• *Siblings*

Richard K. and his older brother Ryan had fought for as long as he could remember. Growing up, he was forced to wear his brother's old clothes, and kids in school always made fun of him. At home, his mother fussed over him. She had tried for more children and wasn't successful, so Richard was the baby. She made sure he got extra servings at dinner because "he was still growing." His mother's preferential treatment did more harm than good. As soon as she was out of earshot, Ryan would lay into Richard, either verbally or physically. He wanted to make sure Richard didn't think he was better than him. Ryan's jealousy destroyed their relationship. Now both in their forties, the brothers have been estranged for more than ten years. Their relationship was destroyed by jealousy and resentment, costing them joy that a healthy brotherly relationship could provide.

• *Children*

Sarah A. couldn't wait to have kids. She had a great job and a fantastic husband, and the couple had recently purchased a house in an exclusive community in Tennessee. She read books, watched shows, and listened to podcasts to learn everything about being a good mother. When she gave birth to Ashley, she was delighted. She enjoyed buying the perfect little dresses and shoes for her baby girl. As Ashley got a little older, Sarah found it more difficult to keep up with the spills, dirt, and accidents that were part of motherhood. She found herself becoming more and more disappointed and frustrated. It seemed whenever Ashley went out, she would lose a shoe or a sock. She couldn't drink anything without spilling it. Even when Sarah gave her a coloring book, she didn't do a good job. Ashley didn't seem to do anything right. It was annoying.

Being a mother was more work than Sarah expected. She tried to correct Ashley, but it didn't make a difference. Her husband complained about her fussing all the time at him and their little girl. Sarah didn't know what to do. She couldn't get Ashley to behave the way she wanted, and she was constantly frustrated. She didn't have the patience for a child like Ashley. Sarah had not been a messy toddler, and she started reading at three years old. She worried that Ashley wasn't going to do well in the world if she didn't get herself together. She hated to admit it, but she didn't really like being a mother. She was constantly disappointed, annoyed, and frustrated with Ashley. She just didn't have the patience she knew she probably needed. She felt guilty and began to resent her daughter. She felt like she was losing everything: money, time, and joy, and even the room for her dreams. She reminisced about life before her little bundle of joy came along and disrupted everything. Sarah's guilt and resentment was stealing her ability to experience the joy of motherhood.

• *Friends*

Marianne S. and Linda P. had been friends since elementary school. They could remember their dates for prom and when they each had their very first kiss. Marianne moved to New York City, studied law, and became an environmental attorney. She married a charming graphic artist and had two children. They enjoyed a life balancing corporate events, gallery openings, and PTA meetings. Linda never married but carried on a long relationship with a married man. While Marianne thought what Linda was doing was wrong, she couldn't figure out a way to get her to stop it. She listened when Linda complained about her married boyfriend canceling plans at the last minute or not sending her a gift for Valentine's Day.

Marianne wanted to end the friendship, but she felt guilty. *How could she walk away from such a long friendship?* After all, Linda wasn't hurting her. Even though she tried to explain that to herself, she knew deep in her heart that she didn't want the friendship anymore. She didn't respect her friend and found her embarrassing. She wondered if Linda had the opportunity, would she steal her husband too? Year after year, she gave Linda her time—and regretted it.

• *Authority Figures*

Harlan M. excelled as a basketball player in college. But his coach came down hard on him, either making him run up and down the bleacher steps or forcing him to do push-ups. He didn't seem to treat the other players that way and seemed to have a problem only with Harlan. It was annoying. Harlan's annoyance and resentment grew over the course of the season, until he finally exploded in a fit of rage on the basketball court in front of spectators. His outburst was shared across multiple social media platforms and earned him a reputation as a hothead. While he was a good player, after his outburst, there weren't as many NBA teams looking at him. He wished he had maintained his cool. The whole situation was embarrassing and upsetting. He couldn't really quantify it, but he was sure that outburst impacted his ability to make money in his chosen field.

II. Driving

Marion C. had a forty-five-minute commute to and from work each day. Living in the Northeast, she often had to drive through snow and ice in the winter. She worked in a high-pressure environment at a major technology company and was often rushing back and forth. One morning she flashed her high beams at the car in front of her in the left lane of the highway. After all, everyone knew you shouldn't be in the fast lane if you wanted to drive slowly. The car moved over, but after she passed, the driver sped up and shot at her through her passenger-side window. Surrounded by shattered glass, she pulled off at the nearest gas station to gather her nerves. Luckily for her, the bullet flew into and out of her car without touching her. Marion was terrified, and it took her a few moments to understand what had happened.

Marion never made it into the office that day. She spent hours talking to the police, the insurance company, and her mechanic. The window replacement was less than a thousand dollars, but the time, trauma, and aggravation was plenty. She has struggled with anxiety and depression since the incident. Now when she drives, she doesn't flash her high beams at other drivers.

Marion is just one example. According to the CDC, approximately thirty-eight thousand people are killed in traffic accidents annually in the United States, resulting in $55 billion in medical and work loss costs.[10] In 2022, there were 141 road-rage shooting deaths. [11] While the cost could have been much higher, Marion still paid a huge price for her moment of impatience. She is left with trauma that costs her everything: time, money, creativity, and joy.

III. Society

You probably have some strong opinions on social issues. You might consider yourself an environmentalist, pro-choice champion, good ol' boy, or a social justice activist. Whatever position you choose, it's easy for the 7 Cranky Cousins to get involved when others disagree with you. It's even worse when that disagreement leads to feelings of oppression.

Monica M. couldn't stand going home for the holidays. No matter how many times she tried to explain to her parents that she was in a relationship with another woman, they wouldn't hear of it. They completely dismissed her and made her fiancée feel terrible. It was ridiculous. She had been dating Sofia for five years, and this year they were finally engaged and planning their wedding. Each time she saw her parents, her annoyance and frustration bubbled over. They knew exactly what to say to trigger her. Monica didn't want to disrespect her parents, so she swallowed her resentment like a lump of hard candy and tried to make it through their visit. She tried over and over again to defend herself and Sofia. *Why couldn't they just be happy for her?* Year after year, nothing changed. Her unhappiness began to chip away at her joy and at the health of her relationship. She was only thirty-five when she developed ovarian cancer. According to the National Institutes of Health, chronic stress can promote cancer development.[12] It's true that that Anger's 7 Cranky Cousins will make you miserable, but they can also make you sick. Monica will never know whether there is a direct link between her cancer and her emotions. What she does know is that all those years of annoyance and frustration stole plenty of time, energy, and joy.

IV. Politics

You are probably convinced your opinion is the "right" one whether you are a conservative, liberal, independent, or something in between. Most people hold political beliefs in a silo, particularly since the advent of social media, internet search engines, and the complex algorithms that run them. As is set forth clearly in films like *Stare into the Lights My Pretties* and *The Social Dilemma*, platforms like Facebook, Google, Instagram, and TikTok send users information that breeds confirmation bias; you are more likely to see material the algorithm thinks you already agree with and that therefore supports your reality.

Herman L. grew up in a small conservative town in the southern United States. His parents drove home Christian values, which included things like "traditional family values," working hard to earn a living, and being a proud American. Herman made his career as an insurance underwriter after a short stint in the US Army. Over the years, he noticed increasing numbers of immigrants coming into his state. He didn't think much about it until his son was laid off from his manufacturing job. It seemed that immigrants were taking all the good jobs away from natural-born US citizens. When he watched the local conservative news or read his Facebook feed, everything he saw gave the same message: Immigration needed to be curtailed. He just couldn't understand why the government kept letting in people from other countries instead of taking care of Americans first.

Herman started complaining to anyone who would listen about the onslaught of illegal immigrants, his son's job loss, and how it just wasn't fair for hardworking Americans. His complaints were rooted in disappointment at his son's job loss, frustration that things didn't seem to be improving in his town, and resentment toward the immigrants he perceived to be taking something away from his family. Even after his son moved on to another job that offered better pay, Herman continued to express his annoyance, frustration, and resentment. He found it difficult to focus on anything else. The woodworking projects he used to enjoy no longer held his interest. He got wrapped up in a subtle web of anger that became a bit of an obsession. His anger and resentment became a time-consuming hobby. Even his son became tired of hearing his father complain about the same issues over and over again. Herman's anger cost him time, joy, and creativity.

V. Losses

Molly C. met Tony during her junior year of college, where she was a film major. Once they found each other, they were inseparable. They got married four years after graduation. The timing was perfect. They were both settled into their careers, and not too long after, they started trying for a baby. Molly conceived easily and was overjoyed. After a few common discomforts during pregnancy, she gave birth to Sarah. Immediately after giving birth, Molly realized that becoming a mother wasn't what she expected. She felt like she lost her freedom and her body in one fell swoop. Sarah seemed to cry constantly, and Molly wasn't getting enough sleep. Tony was rarely home because he traveled a lot for work; when he was home, he wasn't much help. He thought she should feel happy, but she didn't.

Nobody had told Molly that motherhood could feel like a loss. She missed her old life, her figure, her sleep, her career, and her freedom. She was jealous when she saw young, single women going to work or to parties or traveling the world. She knew she wanted to stay home with her baby, but she felt trapped. She felt guilty. Mothers were supposed to be happy—overjoyed, really. She told herself she was stupid and ungrateful. Her disappointment and guilt cycled through her mind daily, wilted her spirit, and stole her joy.

One day, when Molly was heading home from grocery shopping, she looked in the back seat of her car and Sarah wasn't there. Her heart sank into her stomach as she put the car in park. She had left the baby's car seat on the roof of the car! She rushed out of the driver's door and saw the seat rocking back and forth on the roof. She let out a breath: *Holy smokes! Thank God!* Molly looked around, embarrassed and horrified. It was only after this incident that she summoned the courage to share her feelings with a doctor and get treated for postpartum depression. After seeking help and learning to work through her disappointment, guilt, and feelings of loss, she was able to find work that she enjoys and hire a nanny to help with her daughter. She cannot regain the time she spent kicking herself, fighting with her husband, and resenting her daughter. Thankfully, she didn't pay a heavier price.

VI. Choices

Marcia P. grew up in a small, close-knit Jewish family on Long Island, New York. During her teen years she got mixed up with the wrong crowd and started drinking, smoking, and experimenting with drugs. At sixteen, she found herself pregnant after a day of binge drinking and partying with her high school friends on a school field trip to a state park. By the time she realized she was expecting, it was too late to terminate the pregnancy. Her parents offered their support and allowed Marcia to work for the family's accounting business while she raised their grandson. However, they didn't agree to be babysitters, so Marcia dropped out of high school to earn a living and pay for daycare for her child.

As Marcia entered her twenties, she felt like an outcast among her friends. Some of the people she drank and did drugs with never went on to college, but most of them did. She saw social media posts from her old friends who were seemingly living it up in college and then moving on to interesting careers; meanwhile, she was stuck working for her parents. She didn't have much time for dating or fun because she was raising her child alone. In the beginning, her family tried to seek involvement from the father—an acquaintance of one of her high school friends—but they soon decided it wasn't worth the time or trouble to pursue. She did her best to raise her son, but she was unhappy. She was jealous of her friends in college and frustrated with her life, and she often felt guilty for what she felt were her shortcomings as both a mother and a daughter. Even so, she harbored a tinge of resentment toward her parents. *Why didn't they babysit like other grandparents so she could have finished high school and gone on to college?* Her negative emotions and disappointment led her to bouts with depression and anxiety.

At the suggestion of her parents, Marcia got connected with a good therapist who helped her unravel years of entanglement with the Cranky Cousins. She was prescribed medications to alleviate some of her symptoms. However, the root of Marcia's problems was her emotions and how she handled them. She didn't know she had any options. Thankfully, she got help to move her life in a healthier direction for herself and her son. However, she lost years to resentment, guilt, and frustration.

VII. Life in General

Mary D. grew up in a small, rural town in Idaho. From the time she was a little girl, she dreamed of becoming an actress. Her parents thought it was ridiculous, so they discouraged her. She acted in a few school plays in high school, married her high school sweetheart, and put her acting dreams on a shelf. She had a good marriage. Her husband worked as an insurance underwriter, and she stayed home and raised their three children. People thought she had a great life, but she always wondered what her life would have been like if she had gone after her dreams. She was obsessed with celebrity magazines. She sometimes resented her parents for not encouraging her—or at least not discouraging her—to try to follow her dreams. She loved her husband, but she wondered if maybe she got married too young. Sometimes she felt her life was too boring. She longed for the joy she felt from acting. She was tired of being practical. Everything seemed okay, but she wanted to feel more than just okay. Although her resentment and frustration were subtle, they resulted in a chronic case of boredom and disappointment. She just couldn't summon up real joy, despite all the good things in her life.

VIII. Self

Lilibeth M. was frustrated with herself. She was a chronic procrastinator and could never maintain the routines she set for herself. Every week she would set a schedule to get up early and work out, eat a salad at lunchtime, drink a smoothie for dinner, and meditate before going to sleep. She was lucky if she could keep up with her routine three days in a row. Now matter how many books she read about habits, she couldn't make a schedule stick. She was constantly letting herself down and berating herself. She felt like such a loser. Everyone else could maintain a simple schedule. Why couldn't she? The cycle of attempting her desired routine, failing, and being disappointed led to frustration and guilt. She was so unhappy with herself. What was wrong with her?

At the suggestion of a friend, Lilibeth started working with a life coach. She learned to set realistic goals, hold herself accountable, and offer herself some grace when she wasn't perfect. Over time she was able to improve her mental and physical health, treat herself with compassion, and start enjoying her life more.

KEY POINTS

1. Anger is sneaky and shows up in many subtle ways, what I refer to as 7 Cranky Cousins: disappointment (anger about a perceived loss); annoyance (anger about an irritation, often repetitive); frustration (anger about unresolved issues); jealousy (anger about someone else's good fortune); impatience (anger about having to wait); guilt (anger at yourself); and resentment (anger extended over a long time).
2. Like any form of anger, the 7 Cranky Cousins cover for other emotions and transmit incorrect information. Simply put, they lie.
3. Living with anger and its variations is no fun and will sidetrack you from the things you want in your life: time, money, creativity, and joy.

It is normal to experience a range of emotions. However, the faster you can identify and transform negative emotions, the happier and more productive you will become. Over time, you will learn to transition so quickly, you may not experience anger and its 7 Cranky Cousins at all.

That will save you countless amounts of time and energy. Find a quiet space to spend thirty minutes or so working through the material below.

ANGER MYTHBUSTER EXERCISE

Process

1. Grab your journal or electronic device for note-taking.
2. Find a comfortable location in your home or other space. Take a few deep breaths, inhaling through your nose and exhaling through your mouth.
3. Write your answers to the following questions:
   - Which of the 7 Cranky Cousins resonates the most with you?
   - Describe the last time you experienced each of the 7 Cranky Cousins. For each one, explain what happened that you didn't like and the results of this subtle variation of anger, and try to identify the underlying emotion(s).

Practice

- Notice when feelings of anger and its Cranky Cousins arise. When your anger subsides or when you gain awareness of the more subtle feelings of disappointment, annoyance, frustration, jealousy, impatience, guilt, or resentment, reflect on what happened that you didn't like, how the Cranky Cousins make you feel, and any underlying emotions. Write them down.

Chapter 3

Why Ignoring and Repressing Anger Don't Work

Reframing and repressing are two different things.

Isn't it unhealthy to repress anger? Don't you have to let it out? I'm not repressing my anger! That's not good for you! These are some of the most common remarks I hear about anger. Do any of them sound like something you might say? The fact is, most people don't know the difference between learning to get rid of anger and repressing it. The real freedom comes when the things that used to make you angry simply don't bother you anymore. This doesn't mean that you suddenly become a doormat with no feelings or boundaries; it means that by acknowledging your anger and learning to quickly (and gracefully) transform it into either constructive action or peace, you experience little to no anger in your life. It may sound far-fetched, but it is possible with a little bit of time and attention.

Before we get into how magical it will be when you open yourself up to an anger-free world, I want to explain why it is so important to acknowledge and process your anger instead of repressing it. According to the National Institutes of Health, both *expressing* and *repressing* anger can have negative effects on cardiovascular health.[1] This makes sense, when you think about it. You probably remember a time when you got so angry you broke something, got into a heated argument, or even had a physical altercation with someone. Maybe you tried to hold your anger in and ended up with a headache, body aches, or even chest pains. You may have been told to redirect your anger to a pillow, a punching bag, or even strenuous exercise. While this physical release may temporarily redirect your anger, when you are finished punching the pillow, doing a few rounds at the gym with a speed bag, or running a marathon, you will find that the same unresolved emotions are there. You (and your emotions) might be a little exhausted, but after a couple of good nights' rest, the same problem will arise again. The reality is that you never learned to deal with the issue that caused your anger in the first place. **Instead of expressing or repressing it, learning to reframe your anger is the path to clarity, peace, and action.**

REPRESSION VERSUS REFRAMING IN ACTION

Let's once again take a look at the things that might upset us and how repression of anger can play a role.

I. Relationships

Sandra C. grew up in an upper-middle-class home in the suburbs of New York City. She spent years in therapy trying to understand her own identity as the youngest child in an affluent family. She held a lot of resentment toward her parents because she felt her sheltered upbringing was too restrictive and made her feel claustrophobic and self-conscious. She was raised by nannies and didn't get much attention from her busy parents during her formative years. When she became an adult, her parents often used finances to control her, threatening not to provide the party and travel budgets, education assistance, and condo down payments she had come to expect. While she knew she was fortunate, this lifestyle was common among her peers, and the constant pressure to live up to her parents' standards made her feel angry and unhappy in her life. Before she began therapy, her peers often encouraged her to confront her parents with her resentment, which sometimes showed up as snide remarks, small passive-aggressive comments, and even outright sabotage of her mother's appointment calendar or personal items. No matter how many trails she hiked or miles she ran, Sandra struggled with her feelings of anger and disappointment. It wasn't until Sandra began to consider her parents as complex human beings—much like herself—that she found a path to healing.

She learned her mother had grown up with an oppressive and abusive father and had married when she was only nineteen. Her father was an immigrant and grew up in poverty. As she reflected on what she already knew about them and learned to put herself in their shoes, she developed compassion for them. She realized they weren't simply older versions of herself, with all her modern-day resources. They came from another time, another world, and an entirely different educational and cultural system. As Sandra continued to learn and understand more about her parents, she began to respect everything they had to overcome and endure to provide her with the best life they could manage. They clearly had shortcomings, but taking the time to use her imagination, grow her compassion, and reframe her thoughts offered her peace where she once thought none was possible.

II. Driving

When Violet K. was growing up on the Caribbean island of St. Croix, it wasn't very common for women to drive. When she emigrated to the United States she lived in New York City, and, like many New Yorkers, didn't bother to get a license since public transportation was so readily available. When she was in her early fifties, she got her license for the first time to take a job as a nanny for a middle class family in New Jersey. When she was driving around her New Jersey neighborhood, she found that the other drivers could be quite rude and aggressive. They honked at her, rolled their eyes, cut her off, and gave her the finger. She knew she wasn't the most experienced driver on the road, but she was doing her best as a new driver in middle age. Most of the time her embarrassment kept her quiet, but every now and then she swerved the car, slammed on her brakes, or honked in a fit of rage. She nearly caused an accident more than once, and she always felt shame and guilt because of it. It wasn't until she looked at her situation clearly that she accepted the fact that she needed help to become a better driver. She broached the topic with her employers, who were happy to pay for a series of driving lessons to get Violet's driving up to New Jersey standards. Instead of continuing to be angry with other drivers on the road, Violet used her imagination: She thought about how she might appear to the other drivers and realized her driving was not up to par. Although she didn't have extra cash, she got creative and presented the idea to her employers, who were able to pay for her driving lessons. Violet reframed her anger, took constructive action, and changed her situation.

III. Society

When he was a freshman in high school, Kevin L. was a kind and sensitive young man. He enjoyed science fiction and comic books and was adored by his friends as a bit of a nerdy geek. After his first high school relationship ended abruptly, he traded art and comics for beer, parties, and meaningless sex. Based on the movies, TV shows, and influencers he watched, and even conversations with his friends and family, he understood clearly that masculinity involved adventure, alcohol, and as much promiscuity as possible. There was no place for sensitivity, and women weren't to be completely trusted.

As Kevin approached age thirty, he recognized that he wanted a family and children, but he still didn't want to be emotionally vulnerable and expose himself to the possibility of heartbreak. He eventually married, and while he was sure he loved his wife, he often spoke down to her. He made disparaging comments like, "Everyone knows men are better drivers than women," or, "If women had to run the government, they would have to take a week off every month." He complained about his wife's cooking and cleaning skills, even though she worked a full-time job. He saw no problem making sexist jokes with his friends in front of his wife.

It wasn't until his wife had enough and demanded they go to couples therapy that he realized he had never healed the pain or processed the anger from his high school breakup. Messages from society fed into his pain, teaching him that anger, callousness, and alcohol proved he wasn't "weak." Through counseling, he was able to move past his high school heartbreak and reframe the way he looked at his early relationship—and all women. He got curious about the media messages and images he had been absorbing for years. He realized a lot of the influencers he followed offered "clickbait" that riled up his negative emotions but didn't help him grow as a person. Kevin finally took some time to sort through his emotions, understand the impact of negative societal messages, and chart a course to greater compassion for his wife and himself. While he lost a few of his "drinking buddy" friends in the process, this led him to a more fulfilling and loving relationship with his wife and a reconnection to the science fiction and comic books he loved in his teens. Simply ignoring his feelings had put him on a path toward disaster, but reconnecting with who he was before negative societal messages took hold of him gave him his life back.

IV. Politics

Amenah M. was very upset about the US government's pro-Israel political position. As a first-generation Palestinian American, she knew that the Holocaust was an atrocity, but she also felt that her own Palestinian people were overlooked and abused, largely because of their skin color. Amenah worked as a legal aid attorney in New York City. Her colleagues often invited her to lunch, but she always declined. She just didn't feel comfortable with many of her Jewish coworkers. She worried that the topic of Israeli policy might come up, and she didn't know how she would handle it.

Every time she saw a bomb dropped on the Palestinian people or heard about killings in her homeland, she would get so angry. She was certain that if she spoke about it, she wouldn't be understood—people might even accuse her of being racist or anti-Semitic—so she held it all inside.

One day a coworker asked if she heard about the mass shooting at a synagogue in Pittsburgh, Pennsylvania. She mumbled under her breath, "I don't know why this synagogue is getting so much attention when Palestinians are killed every day." Her coworker was horrified. News of her comments spread throughout the legal community. *How could she make such a callous comment during such a devastating time?*

Her manager scheduled a meeting with Amenah to confirm that what he heard was true. Did she really say that? He told her to apologize to her coworker and said that if she was really concerned about Palestine, she should work to help her people and educate others.

The directive from her boss got Amenah thinking. Maybe she could work to benefit her own Palestinian people in a new way. Her family always sent clothes and money back home, but she had never thought about educating people in her community in the United States. She created a small group in her community for Palestinian attorneys to connect, later expanding it to provide education to her coworkers and other local legal office teams.

Her boss's comment got her to think about reframing her anger and led her to take action instead of repressing it and taking the risk it might surface accidentally at the most inappropriate time.

V. Losses

Tish K. drove to an animal rescue in her hometown of Atlanta, Georgia, the same day she signed her divorce papers. Her divorce from her surgeon husband had been long and complicated. They divided property, investment accounts, and the family businesses. She promised herself that when everything was said and done, she would find herself a puppy and focus on growing her interior design firm. She had longed for a little dog over the course of her twenty-six-year marriage, but her husband always refused. When she found a silver-gray miniature schnauzer, she immediately fell in love.

She named the furry little pup Freedom and treated him like her newest baby. Her human kids were all graduated from college and out of the house, so it all made sense to her. Freedom had a designer collar and an extensive wardrobe, and ate only the highest-quality organic food from his crystal bowls.

Tish spent the next ten years curling up on the sofa, taking long walks, and traveling all around the country with Freedom. She had a few boyfriends during that time, but Freedom was her constant companion. She was content. She enjoyed her work, her home, and her family, and she had plenty of time to explore new romantic relationships.

One day she took Freedom for one of their regular walks and noticed blood in his urine. The next few weeks were a whirlwind of vet appointments and hospital stays. Tish was devastated when Freedom finally succumbed to prostate cancer.

Tish thought of herself as a strong woman, so after making reasonable arrangements, she went on with her business and personal life as if nothing happened. Her friends noticed she had become irritable and moody, but Tish refused to talk about Freedom or acknowledge their remarks. She felt let down by the loss of her pup and cheated by his short life. She found herself jealous and resentful of other people whose dogs lived longer lives. She especially hated to see happy couples with their dogs. She didn't understand why Freedom was taken from her when she had already lost her husband and her kids were grown and on their own. She was angry with God.

It wasn't until Tish worked with a grief counselor that she learned she had been burying her anger and pain—not only for the loss of her dog but for the loss of her marriage. The counselor helped her realize how lucky she was to have had a healthy, loving dog for ten years; a good solid marriage for more than twenty years; and a strong career to rely on. The counselor helped her embrace the changes that had taken place in her life without jealousy and resentment. When she learned to reframe her anger, she was able to enjoy the memories of her marriage and her little puppy and to focus on enjoying her work and her friends. She even found that her heart healed enough to welcome a new furry friend into her home.

VI. Choices

Dorothy S. had wanted to be a writer for as long as she could remember. When she was a little girl, she spent hours writing in her diary, taking notes in class, and writing poems. She was an avid reader as well. She loved reading all the stories she could get her hands on. When she was eight years old, she wrote her first short story. By the time she was twelve, she was writing to magazines offering her opinions for the "Letter to the Editor" column. In high school, she edited her school newspaper. When she told her mother she wanted to pursue a career as a writer, her mother smiled and nodded. But when she told her father, he was livid. Her dad, a renowned attorney, expected Dorothy to go to law school and work in the family business. Dorothy knew her father wanted her to be a lawyer, but she didn't think he was so serious that he would demand it of her.

Of course, Dorothy wanted to make her father happy, so she continued her writing as a hobby, studied pre-law as an undergrad, and went on to law school. She interned at a large law firm before coming to work for her father at his estate planning practice. It wasn't long before she realized she had made a terrible decision. She was miserable. She hated everything about being an attorney: the conservative clothes; long, drawn-out documents; and language that nobody could understand. She thought what lawyers did to words should be a crime.

She had spent so many years studying the law to please her father and so many late nights hunched over her computer or in study groups. She had put so much time into it that she couldn't imagine finding another career now. Besides, she knew she would upset her father.

Dorothy was miserable, but she kept quiet. She didn't want to upset her family, so she buried her emotions. Over time she began to grow resentful. *Why had her father pressured her to follow his dreams instead of her own?* Each day she longed for a different career, but she felt stuck. As much as she wanted to blame her father, the fact was that she really needed to blame herself. She was the one who had gone along with his plan. *Why didn't she ever stand up for herself?*

Dorothy kept her head down and did the work she was expected to do. She eventually married and had a child of her own. Then, the day before her forty-fifth birthday, her father died of a massive heart attack. As his only child and heir to his business, she took on sole responsibility for leading the family firm. At her father's funeral, Dorothy was inconsolable, but she wasn't sure it was only because of the tremendous loss; she found herself wailing because she was living a life she didn't want at all. She never wanted to be a lawyer. She did it for her father—she had put her entire life on hold trying to please him—and now he was gone. So what was the point?

When family and friends heard Dorothy wailing, they thought it was because she loved her father so much. They didn't realize it was also because of the choices she'd made that brought her so much misery.

The death of her father made Dorothy come to terms with her own mortality. Life is short. A few years after his death, she sold the firm, split the proceeds with her mother, and began working on a writing career. It took her father's death for her to recognize that she had been stuffing her anger and pain away for years, and his funeral was the eruption.

VII. Life in General

Raymond J. grew up in low-income housing in Brooklyn, New York. For as long as he could remember, every day was hard. The hallways and elevator in his building smelled like urine most of the time. He wasn't allowed to go anywhere without his big brother. He and his brother had to go meet his mom at the bus stop every evening to make sure she got back to their apartment safely. Crime was out of control in their apartment complex, and the police usually didn't come if they were called—or if they did, they took a long time.

Nearly everyone in his building was Black or Hispanic. He knew at least part of the reason life was so hard was because he was Black and his mom was poor. His father was killed when he was in elementary school, so he never really knew him. All he knew was this difficult life—constantly hungry and always in fear.

As he entered his teens, he got more and more angry, but he was a quiet kid so he kept it inside. He didn't like to speak unless he had something important to say. When he was eighteen, he got a job in the mail room at a large Manhattan office building. He mostly liked his job, but he didn't like the way some of the other employees looked at him from time to time. He could tell when they were looking down on him, and he didn't like it.

One day he was sorting mail when Lisa, one of the administrative assistants, came into the mail room looking for a package for her boss. Raymond was having trouble finding her package.

"Come on, Ray Ray, it's got to be here somewhere!" the assistant giggled, but for Raymond it was no laughing matter.

"My name's *not* Ray Ray," he snapped.

"Well, excuuuuse me!" Lisa replied, rolling her eyes. "It's not that serious."

In that moment, Raymond erupted. He slammed a package on the desk and roared, "I'm tired of this fucking place and all the disrespect I have to stomach on a daily basis!" By the time he finished ranting, Lisa was long gone and he was exhausted. *What had come over him? He was usually such a quiet dude.*

Thankfully, no one else was around and Lisa didn't complain about him to his boss. When he got home that evening, he told his mother what happened. She suggested he reach out to their pastor and set up a time to talk.

When Raymond spoke to his pastor that weekend, he learned that his eruption came from anger that had built up over time. Lisa hadn't done anything wrong; she was just the straw that broke the camel's back. The pastor suggested that Raymond learn to process his negative emotions a little at a time instead of keeping them bottled up. He directed Raymond to programs in his community that would give him a place to express himself and make him feel more confident about his future. By speaking to his pastor and joining a job readiness group and a youth leadership program, Raymond learned how dangerous it can be to repress your negative emotions. He was grateful he didn't have to lose his job to learn this lesson.

VIII. Self

Joshua E. was diagnosed with attention-deficit/ hyperactivity disorder (ADHD) when he was ten years old. He struggled through school but managed to graduate from a good state university with a law degree. He did well in his career but had a hard time living up to the goals he set for himself. He would make plans to clean out the garage or his closets, then constantly put it off. He often made promises to take his girlfriend to a concert or movie and then forgot about it. He felt like he couldn't juggle all his goals and the other demands on his time and attention.

Throughout each day, the voice in his head was constantly berating him. All day long, the voice told him, "You're an idiot; you forgot again! Nancy is going to leave you and find another boyfriend," or, "You're such a loser. I don't know what she sees in you. When she figures out what a loser you are, she'll be gone," or, "I don't know how you made it through law school. You barely made it. You're so incompetent." He was angry with himself for failing to meet his own expectations.

Over time, he began keeping to himself more and more. When Nancy asked what was wrong, he pushed her away, and he started spending weekends alone at home instead of with her. He started feeling sad and depressed. Nancy suggested he speak to a therapist.

In therapy, he realized that he hadn't been taking his ADHD diagnosis seriously. He needed more help than other people to follow through on tasks and stay organized. He was able to reframe his anger at himself and cut himself some slack. He had been managing his diagnosis on his own for most of his life and had never given himself credit for all he had been able to accomplish. Once Joshua learned to stop his self-loathing behaviors and reframe the anger he was directing at himself, he got the support he needed to manage his ADHD and enjoy his life.

* * *

Now that you see that repressing and reframing anger are not solutions, it's time to prepare for what is. In the next section, you will be introduced to the five-step Tame and Reframe method for transforming anger. These simple steps, when practiced regularly, can be processed in a fraction of a second, a full minute, or a bit longer depending on your skill level. If you haven't noticed already, it will be easy to remember and implement because the steps themselves spell out the word **ANGER:**

1. **A**cknowledge your anger.
2. **N**otice your breath.
3. **G**ear up your imagination.
4. **E**ntertain, Educate, or Enlighten yourself.
5. **R**ecognize your success.

Like any learned skill, you will get better at transforming and metabolizing your anger over time.

KEY POINTS

1. Both expressing and repressing anger can have negative effects on health.
2. When you repress anger, you don't deal with the issue that caused your anger in the first place.
3. When you express anger, you don't deal with the underlying emotion causing it.
4. Learning to reframe your anger is the path to clarity, peace, and constructive action.

There are many reasons for passionate emotions. However, anger always leads us in the wrong direction, whether we express it outwardly or try to bottle it inside. Find a quiet space to spend thirty minutes or so working through the material below.

ANGER MYTHBUSTER EXERCISE

Process

1. Grab your journal or electronic device for note-taking.
2. Find a comfortable location in your home or other space. Take a few deep breaths, inhaling through your nose and exhaling through your mouth.
3. Write your answers to the following questions:
   - Which examples resonated the most with you?
   - What did they remind you of in your own life?
   - How did those situations play out?
   - Describe the last time you repressed your anger. Did it come out later in a way you didn't expect? Is it still pushed down inside of you?
   - Describe the last time you expressed your anger. What was the underlying emotion (hurt, fear, embarrassment, etc.)? What was the result?

Practice

- Notice when feelings of anger and its 7 Cranky Cousins arise. When your anger subsides or when you gain awareness of the more subtle feelings of disappointment, annoyance, frustration, jealousy, impatience, guilt, or resentment, reflect on your response:
  - Did you repress your anger or express it? Did you do something different?
  - Can you identify what happened that you didn't like (your trigger)? Can you identify the underlying emotions? Write them down.

PART TWO

The Five-Step Solution—
Tame and Reframe

Chapter 4

Acknowledge Your Anger

Trying to use anger for good is like
seasoning your food with poison.

There are concepts that change the path of humanity. Isaac Newton's discovery of gravity, Albert Einstein's theory of relativity, and the understanding that the earth is round and orbits the sun are all life-altering realizations. While understanding the Anger Myth won't change the scientific community, it *will* change your life. In this chapter you will learn the first step in the five-step Tame and Reframe solution: **Acknowledge Your Anger**.

When you recognize anger for what it is—a useless distraction—you can learn to live a life free from its disruption and destruction. To understand how the Anger Myth is different, it's helpful to grasp other theories about anger. It's time for a little anger education.

When faced with an anger trigger,
the first step is to acknowledge your anger.

If you go online and search the question "Is anger useful?" you will find a stream of articles explaining the merits of anger. Before we look at some of the most common proposed benefits of anger, one by one, consider the difference between being outraged and being enraged. If you consult a dictionary, it's difficult to make a distinction between the two based on their definitions. However, the words themselves hold keys—the difference between "out" and "in." If you see injustice or violence, you may find what you observe to be troubling and offensive and can make the decision to intervene or take some constructive action. You are outraged. However, if you witness some type of trigger, instead of being an observer, you incorporate anger into your being. You are engulfed by your anger and under the influence of it, becoming enraged. You cannot think clearly until you are no longer at the mercy of your rage. **To be outraged is to have some mental space between you and your anger. To be enraged is to have none.**

In either case, it's important to acknowledge your anger. As you learned in Chapter 3, ignoring or repressing anger can create all kinds of problems, and you can't work through what you don't recognize. If you want to free yourself from the pain and destruction of anger, the first step is to acknowledge it. Anger isn't your enemy or your savior. You are human, and anger is a feeling that can arise. When it does, your first step is simply to notice it. That's it! Just notice your anger as if it were a speck of lint on your jacket. It's there, but it's not useful. **Much like a broken clock will tell the right time twice per day, anger is the most inefficient way to accomplish anything.** Resorting to anger is like hammering a nail with a battering ram and patting yourself on the back for a job well done, or seasoning food with antifreeze and relishing its sweet taste. It may seem to work initially, but it creates additional problems. You would do far better picking up an effective tool or adding wholesome sweeteners into your life. With this understanding, here are some of the common misbeliefs about anger.

COMMON MISBELIEFS ABOUT ANGER[1]

Misbelief #1: Anger Helps Us Survive

The misbelief that anger is helpful to survival comes from the idea that anger prepares you to fight. While this might have made sense in caveman days when our understanding of ourselves and our surroundings was very rudimentary, it hardly applies in modern times. Many of the best fighters teach how anger hinders fight performance.

Bruce Lee, arguably the greatest martial artist of the twentieth century, once said, "The most dangerous person is the one who listens, thinks, and observes."[2] When you give in to anger, your ability to think and process information is immediately disrupted. Heavyweight boxing champion Mike Tyson's legacy is full of moments of anger, including a street fight at the height of his boxing career in 1988 and the infamous

1997 match when he bit off a piece of Evander Holyfield's ear. In 2020, Tyson wrote on Instagram, "Everybody thinks this is a tough man's sport. This is not a tough man's sport. This is a thinking man's sport. A tough man is gonna get hurt real bad in this sport." This man, who some would think benefited from anger in his career, said, "Anger is my biggest enemy in life."[3] And going as far back as the sixth century BCE, ancient Chinese philosopher Lao Tzu, founder of Taoism, said, "The best fighter is never angry."[4]

Even for prize fighters, anger isn't necessary to survive. First acknowledge your anger, then prepare to transform it.

Misbelief #2: Releasing Anger Is Calming

The misbelief that anger is calming stems from the idea that anger expression is useful. You learned in Chapter 3 that this is not the case. Expressing anger can cause a host of problems. Yelling, screaming, hitting, and throwing things are all forms of release that are destructive. You might damage property, harm others, or hurt yourself. You cannot do anything constructive until *after* you transform your anger.

Rage rooms and "Dammit dolls" are part of a trend to release anger in a controlled, nonharming environment. (If you haven't heard of them, Dammit dolls are stuffed dolls designed to be banged against a wall when you are angry, while you yell "Dammit!") However, these tactics may have the undesirable effect of glamorizing violence and aggression.[5] The reality is that businesses that offer these products and services may capitalize on people's frustrations, but they do not provide any solution. Anger cannot be resolved unless it is acknowledged and transformed.

Exercise can be a placeholder. Going for a run or a workout as a temporary means to release energy and produce mood-lifting endorphins can be very helpful. Exercising gives your body something constructive to do while giving your mind time to process your emotions. However, simply releasing anger in and of itself isn't calming or helpful; learning to process and reframe your anger is.

Misbelief #3: Anger Helps Us to Maintain Control

One of the most troubling problems with anger is that it can make you *feel* in control when the opposite is true—you are actually out of control. As we discussed in Chapter 1, anger is a deluded mindset that exaggerates, so when you are angry, you cannot see clearly or make sound decisions. You may have had moments of anger where you acted impulsively, like shoving or yelling. Or you may have strategically planned action over time, like a revenge plot to get back at an ex or an old coworker. Either way, anger wants to harm. You will never see a very angry person wishing to spread love and cheer. It's not possible. Anger may make you want to take control of people, things, and situations that are not yours to control. Anger doesn't increase your control over yourself or anyone else.

Only learning to reduce and reframe your anger can give you control over your life. You will reduce thoughtless decisions rooted in negativity and begin making thoughtful decisions from a positive state of mind. Without the hot, disruptive winds of anger, you can pursue the job, education, and relationships that make you feel most stable and satisfied.

Misbelief #4: Anger Is a Great Energizer

If you are in the habit of repressing your emotions, just about any emotion can make you feel energized. Anger is more energizing than sadness, for example, because when you are angry your body releases adrenaline, the fight-or-flight hormone. But as we discussed in Chapter 1, anger can make you feel empowered right at the moment you are most apt to make poor decisions. Don't trust that jolt of energy; it will lead you in the wrong direction. You can probably remember many misguided decisions you made when anger suddenly overcame you. You might have blurted out words that got you into trouble, driven recklessly, made a hasty phone call to give someone a piece of your mind, or even started a fight.

If you really want to be energized, reduce the time you spend being angry and learn to be happier. Happiness is the real energy boost. As you move through the chapters in this book, you will learn techniques to improve your mental and physical health and give you an extra jolt of the right kind of energy.

Misbelief #5: Anger Is a Good Motivator to Reach Your Goals

Some people are motivated by anger; others are motivated by love or justice or compassion. You can choose what motivates you. Why would you choose something that jeopardizes both your physical and mental health and can lead you to a wide range of negative outcomes? Much like the concept of the carrot and the stick, you can choose to be motivated by something positive that enhances your life, like the carrot, versus something negative that harms you, like the stick. It's up to you. Using anger for motivation is like beating yourself with a stick. It's like using cocaine to help you wake up. There are better ways to move yourself forward that aren't damaging and toxic.

If you have goals you want to reach, there are many ways to get excited and stay on track. You could create a strategy, work with a coach or accountability partner, and leverage your relationships with mentors and friends. Follow blogs and podcasts, watch videos, or read books from motivational teachers that inspire you. Create a vision board and learn to visualize achieving your goals. The list of positive ways to pursue your goals is endless. Anger is always the worst possible choice.

Misbelief #6: Anger Is a Prime Way to Fight Injustice

At the beginning of this chapter, I introduced the idea of "outrage" versus "enrage." In the United States, there are regular mass killings, school shootings, kidnappings, rapes, assaults, and police brutality—all of which can make you angry. The country still struggles with its history of colonialism, slavery, and oppression alongside a legacy of racism, sexism, homophobia, transphobia, xenophobia, colorism, classism, ageism, ableism, and all manner of injustices. Global wars and violence seem to be never-ending. It's natural to experience outrage when you witness injustice or atrocities. The challenge is to keep from internalizing the outrage and becoming enraged.

You *can* fight for justice from a place of love. To do this, you must make a commitment to understanding the Anger Myth and implementing the strategies in this book. Whether you are a social justice activist or just a concerned citizen, this requires self-care and effort. This might look like quiet time for contemplation, hobbies, reading, exercise, coaching, therapy, or even a warm bath at the end of a day of protests, vigils, social media campaigns, community meetings, or other justice work.

Fighting harmful and oppressive policies and ideologies isn't easy, whether that means standing up to racist family members or speaking at community rallies. However, you *can* fight for justice in all ways without the harmful effects of internalized anger and rage.

Misbelief #7: Anger Promotes Cooperation

Some people feel that anger communicates to others that it is important to listen to them. On the surface, this can seem true. Anger often leads us to raise or deepen our voices and to yell with heightened emotion. Without access to any other tools, yelling might be your best way to be heard. If you are like most people, yelling doesn't make you listen better. It may even make you stop listening. We live in a modern society with advanced language and access to information about sociology, psychology, and group dynamics. You are not a caveman in the woods holding a club. You have access to much more effective modes of communication and state-of-the-art tools. Just as you don't have to hunt or gather berries to make a healthy, home-cooked meal, you don't have to be angry to communicate clearly and garner cooperation.

When we communicate with anger, the opposite of cooperation is usually the result. Verbal abuse can be defined as "the repeated improper and excessive use of language to humiliate someone, or to undermine someone's dignity."[6] When communicating with emotionally healthy people with intact personal boundaries, showcasing anger will not likely achieve your desired result. Plus, it renders you out of control. Remember that anger lies—you cannot trust the way you process information when you are angry.

"Emotional wellness" can be defined as the ability to successfully handle life's stresses and difficulties, build and maintain meaningful relationships, and adapt to change.[7] Emotionally healthy people will respond better to healthy communication and negotiations. Learning to address issues calmly and objectively with a clear mind is the best way to resolve any conflicts and find mutually beneficial solutions. Learning active listening and communication skills can help build understanding and bridge any gaps between involved parties. If emotions get in the way, it is best to take a break and return to the conversation when everyone is feeling calmer.

Misbelief #8: Anger Improves Business Negotiations

Anger may appear to improve negotiations in business because it imparts fear; however, it is not a sound long-term strategy. And of course, it's a terrible strategy for personal health and good relationships. You may have experienced this type of situation in your own life, either through your own behavior or witnessing it in others. Perhaps you ordered a coffee at a coffee shop and the server delivered the wrong item. Yelling and demanding a replacement and a refund would probably provide a short-term fix. The server would give you what you want to get you to leave the establishment (and not come back).

Another example may look something like this: A senior executive at a large corporation wants to negotiate with materials vendors for the lowest possible pricing. The executive meets with each vendor individually, hearing about the various features and benefits of their offerings. Without fail, at the end of each presentation, the executive slams his hand down on the conference room table, raises his voice, and billows, "This is garbage! I know you can do better!" He is known in the industry as "tough," and because of his purchasing power he is able to use intimidation to get lower pricing—or so he thinks.

It's worthwhile to bring attention to the difference between anger and the appearance of anger here. Much like in a poker game, with practice, using techniques that appear to be anger can sometimes be helpful in situations where access to elevated communications and listening skills is unavailable. According to the APA, anger is most helpful in negotiations with people you will never meet again.[8] If we go back to the example of the rude patron at the coffee shop, the owner of the shop may come out and yell, "Take your refund and don't come back here again!" The owner can use yelling as a performative technique to display anger to someone who only knows how to communicate that way, communicating her message without actually upsetting herself, her staff, or her environment.

Anger, or the appearance of anger, can be used to intimidate and bully during business negotiations. This might lead to desired outcomes;

however, anger isn't the best way to negotiate for a successful business exchange. It damages both business and personal relationships. In the coffee shop example, a simple request would have easily changed the outcome. In the example with the corporate executive, there are myriad books on negotiating strategies that don't involve yelling and bullying.

If you want to improve business negotiations, your best course of action is to improve your communication skills. Anger only adds to the problem.

Misbelief #9: Anger Is a Good Way to Manage Painful Emotions

As you learned in Chapter 1, anger occurs when things don't happen the way you want them to and is always a cover for another emotion, usually some variation of pain coupled with a misguided sense of self-importance. While covering painful emotions can be necessary in the short term—you don't want to cry at work, for example—in the long term, hiding and suppressing painful emotions is unhealthy. As discussed in Chapter 3, the distinction between suppressing anger and reframing it is a big one.

Even in the example of not wanting to cry at work, anger is never helpful because it harms the person experiencing it. For example, if your boss bullies you to the verge of tears, an angry outburst will not help you. Your best solution may be to go to the bathroom to take a breather, blow your nose, and regain your composure. Allow yourself some time to process your emotions away from your coworkers. After you regain your composure, perhaps at the end of the day, you can begin to look for strategies to deal with your abusive boss, such as scheduling a meeting with his superior or human resources. If the situation cannot be rectified, it may be time to consider new employment or find other ways to create space for you to reframe your anger and move toward constructive action.

Humans, like other animals, want to avoid pain. This is not unique. However, avoiding difficult emotions by masking or repressing them creates more problems than solutions. Working through difficult feelings and tackling problems head-on is the most effective way to elevate your emotions and improve your life. You will learn to do this with more finesse as you continue to work through the Anger Myth methods introduced in upcoming chapters.

Misbelief #10: Anger Is a Good Way to Become More Self-Aware

Becoming angry and staying in the feeling of anger is not a good strategy to enhance self-awareness. However, paying attention to the events that trigger your anger and learning to respond in new ways is an incredible personal growth and learning journey. Noticing all of your emotions—negative or positive—will build self-awareness. With attention and conscious adjustments, over time you can increase your positive emotions and reduce the negative ones.

But what is self-awareness? A 2018 study from the *Harvard Business Review* identified two broad categories of self-awareness: internal and external.[9]

Internal self-awareness represents how in tune you are with your own values, judgments, passions, goals, and aspirations. It deals with how well you fit into your environment and your reactions, including thoughts, feelings, behaviors, strengths, weaknesses, and impact on others. High internal self-awareness correlates with increased satisfaction with work and relationships, self-control, social reputation and impact, and happiness. Internal self-awareness decreases the likelihood of anxiety, stress, and depression. For example, suppose a woman tells her partner, "You are the biggest idiot I've ever met." To a self-aware and confident partner who knows they're not an idiot, the words might be alarming but they don't impact their sense of self-worth. However, a partner who doesn't have a keen sense of who they are might fly off the handle. Their anger may make them realize they are triggered when they are referred to as an idiot, but it's a terrible way to gain that self-awareness.

External self-awareness means understanding how other people view you through the same factors listed above. How people perceive your passions, goals, aspirations, behaviors, and so on. According to the research, people who understand how others interpret their behavior are more capable of showing empathy and listening to the perspectives of others. Using the previous example of the woman name-calling her partner, a person with external self-awareness not only knows they're not at idiot, but they also have a good sense of whether their partner really believes they are. In this case, the partner is probably angry and saying damaging and hurtful things they don't actually mean. A person with external self-awareness who doesn't rise to their anger would realize that.

Anger is flawed in every way. It's a terrible way to achieve self-awareness. Reading books like this one and others, building and nurturing relationships, and working with a coach or therapist are much more effective strategies. You don't need to lean into anger to become self-aware.

* * *

There are no benefits to using anger as a strategy. It will destroy everything in its path, including you. This first step to the five-step Tame and Reframe approach is simply to **Acknowledge Your Anger**. Don't follow it. Don't lean into it. Just acknowledge the feeling that arises and get ready for the next step—**Notice Your Breath**—which we will explore in Chapter 5.

KEY POINTS

1. Step one of the five-Step Tame and Reframe technique is **Acknowledge Your Anger**. If you want to free yourself from anger, you must acknowledge it when it arises. Don't give it a lot of attention, but rather a quick "I see you" and recognize it as the time-wasting, destructive feeling that it is.
2. There is a difference between being outraged and being enraged. To be outraged is to have some mental space between you and your anger. To be enraged is to have none. Outrage is a healthy reaction to atrocities and negative situations. Becoming enraged internalizes anger and is not a healthy option.
3. There are many common misbeliefs about anger that create confusion. They may make you think your anger is useful when it is not. Anger is as useful as a broken clock. While anger may indirectly redirect behavior in a positive way, it is never the best choice.

As humans, it is our pleasure and our purpose to experience a wide range of emotions. There are many reasons for passionate emotions. When you understand the Anger Myth, you embark on a journey of greater satisfaction, happiness, and success in life. **You understand for the first time that anger is *never* useful.** It's like dropping a rock on your toe and saying it was helpful because it gave you the awareness of the importance of your foot. *Ouch!* There are better ways to improve yourself and reach new levels of enjoyment in your life without harming yourself in the process.

ANGER MYTHBUSTER EXERCISE

Process

1. Grab your journal or electronic device for note-taking.
2. Find a comfortable location in your home or other space. Take a few deep breaths, inhaling through your nose and exhaling through your mouth.
3. Write your answers to the following questions in a notebook or journal:
   - Which examples of the "usefulness" of anger resonated the most with you?
   - What did they remind you of in your own life?
   - How did those situations play out?
   - Describe the last time you convinced yourself that anger was helpful. Do you still feel the same way now? What might you have done differently to have achieved a better outcome?
   - Describe the last time you expressed your anger. What was the underlying emotion (hurt, fear, embarrassment, etc.)? What was the result?

Practice

- Notice when feelings of anger and its 7 Cranky Cousins arise. Take a moment to acknowledge your anger without immediately responding to it. Say to yourself, "I notice my anger." See if you can say it three times slowly before taking any action.

- When your anger or its 7 Cranky Cousins subside, how do you feel?
- Can you identify what happened that you didn't like (your trigger)? Can you identify the underlying emotions? Write them down.

Chapter 5

Notice Your Breath

Acknowledge your anger first, then breathe.

In the last chapter, you were introduced to the first step in the five-step Tame and Reframe technique for transforming anger: **Acknowledge Your Anger**. In this chapter, you will learn the second step: **Notice Your Breath**. The average adult breathes about twenty thousand times per day.[1] Despite this fact, you probably don't pay much attention to your breathing unless you are sick with a cold or dealing with allergies that make breathing difficult. You probably know that when you breathe you bring oxygen into your body as fuel and release carbon dioxide as waste. This ongoing practice is necessary for survival; the average person can hold their breath for only thirty to ninety seconds before the body forces another breath.[2]

There is great value in bringing your awareness to your breath. While you breathe all day long, you may not know how important the breath is in regulating not only physical health, but also mental health. Your breath is a powerful tool in managing your emotions.

**When faced with an anger trigger, after
first acknowledging your anger,
the next step is to notice your breath.**

In the study of yoga, breathwork, or pranayama, is the practice of focusing on your breath using various breathing techniques. The easiest technique to employ as an immediate response to a feeling of anger is a simple, cleansing breath. You have already taken cleansing breaths as you worked through the Anger MythBuster Exercises in the previous chapters. It is quite easy: simply take a long, deep breath, inhaling through the nose as you let your belly fill, then exhale through the mouth with a sigh. The louder, fuller, and deeper the sigh, the better. You may find yourself in an environment where a loud sigh might be awkward. Just keep in mind that no matter how you access your breath—sigh or no sigh—it will be very helpful.

You might wonder, if you are breathing all day anyway, how does stopping to take a few deep breaths help in taming your anger? There are a number of reasons for this:

1. **Deep breathing gives you something to do.** It's that simple. Instead of automatically going with a habitual response like yelling, honking, or even rolling your eyes, deep breathing gives your mind an activity to focus on.
2. **Deep breathing brings oxygen to the brain.** A few deep breaths will bring additional nourishment to your brain and your body. This helps to ensure that your brain and body are nourished so you can make your next decision with more clarity.
3. **Deep breathing calms your nervous system.** Deep breaths send a message to your body that you are okay. This practice will make you feel more relaxed and able to more intelligently plan your next action.

Let's revisit the things that can make us angry and see how incorporating a few simple breaths can change the trajectory of your day.

THE POWER OF YOUR BREATH IN ACTION

I. Relationships

Miriam L. had been caring for her elderly mother for ten years. Each year was more difficult than the last, as her mother's Alzheimer's disease has progressed. In the first few years, her mother was endearing. She couldn't remember the words for common items like keys or shoes, and she would often break into song or dance, but she was kind and sweet. As her disease progressed, however, her mother became louder and more argumentative. She would yell at Miriam to leave her alone and sometimes even throw her food at her. As much as Miriam knew she shouldn't respond, sometimes she couldn't help herself.

Miriam and her mother didn't have the best relationship. As a child, her mother was prone to binge drinking. Miriam couldn't count the number of times she came home from school and found her mother passed out on the living room sofa. Sometimes her mother screamed and threw canned vegetables at her in a fit of rage. Most of the times Miriam ducked, but once a can hit her right in the temple; she still has a small scar that bears witness to the memory. But despite all that, Miriam loved her mother. She wasn't perfect, but she took care of her daughter as best she could. As an only child, it was left to Miriam to take care of her mother. Usually, she could put any feelings of resentment to the side, but every now and then her mom would say something that cut her to the bone.

"You've always made bad decisions," her mother started one day. "First that terrible husband, then you moved sooo far from your family; I never see my granddaughter."

Here we go again, Miriam thought. Half the time, her mother could barely remember who she was. But when she did, she had nothing good to say.

Miriam ignored her and continued to put white daisies in a clear glass vase at the nursing home where her mother resided.

"I never wanted a baby. I was so young. I wasn't ready."

Miriam said nothing.

"Then you came into my life and fucked everything up!" her mother growled.

Miriam felt the blood rush to her head. Her eyes shot over to her mother, who was sitting in the green recliner next to her bed.

"Yeah, I said it; it was you who fucked my life up!"

Miriam walked out of the room, leaned her back against the wall, and inhaled deeply through her nose, then exhaled. She walked to the lounge area and took a seat. She rubbed her palms together until they generated some heat. Then she placed her right hand on her heart and her left hand on her belly. She was grateful nobody else was in the lounge with her to see her unusual posture. Then she inhaled three times, each time inhaling through the nose and exhaling through the mouth with an audible sigh. She took care not to be too loud because although the room was empty, she was still in a public place.

With some space to think and a few moments of clarity, she reminded herself that her mother was sick. And even if her mom felt that having a child when she was only sixteen ruined her life, she had raised Miriam pretty well—well enough that she had a good career as a project manager, a nice home, and a healthy child. She was okay. Yelling at her mother or expressing her anger in some other way would not change anything. In her breaths, she found a bit of space and a well of compassion for the woman who, though deeply imperfect, brought her into this world.

When Miriam returned to her mother's room, her mother greeted her: "Hi, sweetie!"

II. Driving

Jaleel S. began driving trucks right after he graduated high school. After driving local delivery trucks for a few years, he graduated to the big rigs, driving an eighteen-wheeler for a large delivery company. On most days, he was a calm and conscientious driver. He had a wife and three kids at home who depended on his income. While he hated being on the road for too long, he enjoyed the freedom of being on the road, and he loved driving big rigs.

Jaleel was driving through Mississippi on a long run when another large truck pulled up alongside him. It seemed as if the driver was trying to say something to him, which was strange. Usually truck drivers communicate via CB radio or other means when they are on the road. He couldn't make out what the trucker was trying to say, so he assumed he had made a mistake in thinking he was trying to communicate with him and continued along his journey.

Next thing he knew, the truck passed him at high speed. As a truck driver, he was required to observe the speed limit. The average weight of a tractor trailer with its cargo is eighty thousand pounds, making it very difficult to stop when in motion. (In comparison, the average weight of a passenger vehicle is only four thousand pounds.) Sometimes Jaleel went over the posted limit to keep up with the flow of traffic, but this driver sped past him as if he were in a race car. When Jaleel saw how fast the truck was going, he was shocked.

Jaleel maintained his speed and noticed that the truck ahead of him had slowed down. Now he was getting ready to pass the truck that had just whizzed by him. As he passed, he turned his head to look at the driver. A sunburned man in a Confederate cap looked his way, shoved his middle finger up in the air, and sped off.

Jaleel instantly got hot. *Was he kidding?* He angrily pressed his foot on the gas in an instinctive effort to speed up to the insulting idiot in the long gray truck. Then he remembered to take a breath. He eased his foot off the gas and inhaled, long and deep, through his nostrils. He realized that arguing with a stranger would be a waste of time. He could lose his job or even his life. He exhaled loudly in the truck by himself. As Jaleel took a few more deep breaths, he could feel the calm come over him. It would be ridiculous to lose all that he had worked for because of one miserable driver. He moved his truck into the right lane and continued to cruise safely toward his destination.

III. Society

Adeola L. loved her six-figure job working as a curator for a large metropolitan museum. She enjoyed a fantastic group of friends and exciting hobbies. She enjoyed rock climbing and ran the New York City Marathon more than once. She loved visiting galleries and had beautiful paintings throughout her trendy urban apartment. She was dating a smart, funny, and creative woman and thought she might be falling in love. It seemed like everything was going right for her, but it was never enough.

Beginning when she turned thirty, her Nigerian parents began hounding her to get married and have children. She hadn't dared to tell them she was gay. You would have thought by now they could have figured it out. For goodness' sake, she'd never brought a boyfriend home in all her thirty years! But her family chose to keep their eyes closed. She knew they were homophobic, and she didn't know how to break the news to them.

And even though she lived in a big city, Adeola still got strange looks when she walked down the street with her girlfriend. Sometimes people were wide-eyed. Sometimes they raised their eyebrows. Sometimes they just looked away. Then there were the guys who licked their lips and looked her up and down as if they could imagine wedging themselves into a threesome. *Yuck!*

She had liked girls for as long as she could remember. She was a good member of society. She went to school, got a good job, worked, and paid her taxes. She even gave money to charity and helped her family when they needed her. *Why wasn't that enough?!* On most days she was exhausted. On some days she was infuriated.

She didn't think anything of it when her parents invited her home to celebrate her thirtieth birthday. Birthday celebrations were a big part of her upbringing, and she was ready for the traditional stew with cake, champagne, and lots of music and singing. However, this birthday was different. After her father made a toast, he started, "So, you are thirty now, Adeola, when are you going to get serious about your life?"

"What do you mean, Dad?"

"I mean your mother wants grandchildren."

Adeola looked over at her mother, her face hot. Her mother nodded her head in agreement. Adeola wanted to run far away. Her younger sister looked down and giggled.

"It's true. You don't want to be an old maid," her mother said.

"Old maid, Mom? Seriously?" Adeola whipped her head around. "What the"—she paused before she could drop the f-bomb on her parents. She took a breath. She wanted to tell them to shut up. She wanted to tell them they didn't know the first thing about her. She wanted to tell them that she'd done everything they wanted and they still weren't happy. But instead she left the dining room and headed to the bathroom. She knew she needed to have a conversation with her parents, but now was not the time. She took another breath. She didn't know why she was born this way. She didn't know why her culture couldn't accept people like her. She kept breathing.

When she came back from the bathroom, she laughed the comments off. "You two will be the first to know when I find my husband."

Her parents smiled and nodded.

After dinner, she met up with her girlfriend and told her story to empathetic ears. She wasn't sure how serious their relationship was, but she knew it was time to finally have a conversation and come out to her parents. She probably should have done it a long time ago. That evening, she made a plan to finally tell her parents she was gay.

IV. Politics

Veronica C. had been teaching sixth grade in a small school in the southern United States for nearly thirty years when she was told that going forward, all the books in her classroom had to be reviewed by a media specialist before she used them with her students. She was told to remove all the books from her classroom until the review was completed. She was devastated. Her classroom was full of classic books that she had been sharing with her sixth graders for years. It seemed as if suddenly books were under attack if they had even the mildest messages about racism or sexuality.

She remembered reading coming-of-age classics like Judy Blume's *Are You There God? It's Me, Margaret* and *Forever* when she was growing up. Those books provided information that her parents were too reserved to share with her. She thought it was outrageous that the schools wanted to go back in time and be more conservative than they were when she was growing up more than forty years ago. It was downright Orwellian! Wasn't freedom of speech a right?! She was teacher, for God's sake—she should be able to teach! What was she supposed to tell the children?

At the end of the school day, she finally began packing up her books. It was painful to believe this was the state of education in the United States. As she was packing, a coworker poked her head through the doorway. "It's about time!" she said.

"About time for what?"

"About time they got us to clean up some of this woke agenda crap!"

Veronica's head spun so fast she nearly hurt her neck. "What did you say?"

"I don't know about you, but I'm glad I don't have to teach all that racist nonsense. Kids don't need to be told they are bad."

Veronica's heart started to race. "You think teaching kids the real history of this country and letting them read from diverse authors is bad?"

"Oh, don't get your panties all in a bunch. I didn't mean anything by it."

Veronica took a step forward. For a split second, she wanted to grab the other woman by the shoulders and shake her. How could she be so happy about something that caused Veronica so much pain? She reached out for the woman's shoulders, fingers curled, eyes intent. Just as she brushed the soft rayon of her coworker's blouse, she paused. Her hands dropped to her sides. She took a breath. This was about to go south really fast. She inhaled again. She didn't want to lose her job, and this woman couldn't change policy.

Veronica stepped back. *That was a close call.* In that moment, she decided to do whatever was necessary to fight this policy. If she had placed her hands on her coworker, she would have far bigger problems than banned books.

V. Losses

Trina M., in her job as a public health advocate, flew often, both nationally and internationally, teaching university students and presenting at public health forums. When she boarded her flight to India, she was sure she had all her personal items with her. It wasn't until she was in the air that she realized she was missing the bag that held customer files, her portable charger, and the clicker she used to advance slides during her presentations. *How is this possible?* she wondered. She had counted her bags over and over at the airport, almost to the point of obsession. Forgetting something—especially something she really needed—was her worst nightmare. She started to feel sick. She hit the button to summon the flight attendant.

A tall, slim woman approached her. "How can I help you?"

"I can't find my bag!"

"Okay, calm down. Do you think it's on the plane or at the airport?"

Did that woman just tell me to calm down? How can I calm down? My client files contain private information! she thought. "I'm not sure," she said aloud.

"Oh, well, I don't know where to look if you're not sure." With that, the woman spun on her heel and walked away.

Trina was fuming. *What kind of customer service was that?* She got out of her seat and followed the flight attendant down the aisle of the plane.

"Can I help you?" the attendant asked.

"Yes, you can help me! I told you I *need* help!" Trina was beginning to raise her voice; then she remembered what she had been taught. She paused and took a deep breath before continuing. Now her voice was calm. "I'm just worried because I can't find my bag. Is there a way to check to see if it was misplaced on the plane?"

The flight attendant helped her to look for her bag on the plane, but they couldn't find it. Trina had to make do without some important personal items. The items were already missing by the time Trina got upset. By pausing to take a few breaths, she kept an already-bad situation from becoming much worse.

VI. Choices

Samantha K. was making her famous vegan macaroni and cheese for Sunday dinner at her house. It was so good that her friends and family didn't even realize there was no cheese in it. When she started preparing her special cheesy sauce, she realized she didn't have the main ingredient: nutritional yeast. She jumped into her car and drove to her local supermarket to quickly grab the missing item. That Sunday, it seemed like everyone in Atlanta was doing their grocery shopping. All the lines were long. She found the shortest one and stood in it. But almost as soon as she got there, the woman at the front of the line started asking questions about a package of cookies. The cashier left to go check the shelves.

Samantha switched to a different line that looked like it was moving faster. As soon as she got into that line, the man at the front of the line pulled out a checkbook. *Is he serious?* she thought. *Nobody writes checks anymore!* She looked at her watch. It shouldn't take this long to buy one item from the store! She could feel her face getting flushed. All she wanted was *one* item!

She was switching to yet another line when she saw that the first line had moved forward and the person who had been behind her in line was now checking out. She felt like slamming the container of seasoning on a shelf and storming out of the store. *Are you kidding?*

Just then, an elderly lady tapped her on the shoulder. "Excuse me, miss."

Samantha spun around and was just about to scream at the unsuspecting old woman when she caught herself. She took a breath and waited an extra moment.

The old lady wrinkled her eyebrows.

Samantha took another deep breath. *Calm down, Samantha. It's not that serious.* "Yes?" she said to the woman.

"Do you know where the spices are?"

Samantha chuckled to herself. Yes, she did. She just didn't know how she was ever going to check out from the store. She pointed the woman in the right direction, got back in line, and played a game on her phone until the cashier was ready for her. She knew that if she hadn't paused to breath for a moment, she might have tossed her seasoning, yelled at an old lady and probably a couple of store workers, made herself—and everyone around her—feel terrible, and probably have ended up with her picture on the wall in the breakroom.

She went home and made her famous vegan mac and cheese, and everyone enjoyed it. As it turned out, she had plenty of time.

VII. Life in General

Afia worked as a secretary for a small construction company. She had been married to her husband Kofu for nearly twenty years, and they had five children together. She loved her family, but many mornings she woke up with a knot in her stomach. *Was this all there is to life?* The family lived in a lovely home in a safe neighborhood in the suburbs. Her children all got a good education. Two were already in pre-med programs in college. They socialized with a few couples who were also immigrants from their home country of Ghana. It seemed they had everything they could desire, but Afia still felt something was missing.

One morning, as Afia was preparing boxed lunches for her husband and herself, she was struck with a wave of resentment. Her husband worked as an engineer and always loved the numbers and metrics involved in his career. He had wanted that for as long as she could remember. Although they had been married only twenty years, they had known each other since they were children. When she thought back on their life together, it seemed he got everything he wanted and her only role was to support him. She never wanted to be a secretary. She just took a simple job to help the family. She had trained as an attorney in Ghana but was never able to translate her skills to working in law in the United States. She worked in an office where people thought she was less important than the managers because hers was a support role. They thought she was less intelligent, too.

Afia knew she had no one to blame but herself. She enjoyed supporting her husband and her children; she just wanted to time for herself as well. It seemed everyone was living out their dreams except for her.

"My goodness, Afia, what's taking you so long?" Kofu's tone was inquisitive, not harsh at all.

Afia's stomach tightened. She snapped her head around. She wanted to scream at him about all the sacrifices she had made for their family. She wanted to scream about every time someone dismissed her as being unimportant. She wanted to scream because she was now watching her own children begin to surpass her. She wanted to scream because she was watching her husband pursue his dreams while she worked as a secretary and didn't pursue her own. She locked eyes with her husband. She wanted to scream and throw the potato salad, watermelon, and avocado toast that she had prepared directly at his head.

Afia wanted to scream, but instead she inhaled. She took a long, deep breath. She looked into her husband's eyes and saw his confusion. She took another breath. His eyes went from a question to concern. Afia took another breath and sat down.

Kofu sat next to her. "Are you okay?"

"I think I need some help."

He was silent.

"I don't think I know who I am anymore."

Kofu's eyebrows raised.

"I need to figure some things out." Afia made the decision to get some help to figure out what she could do to change the things in her life that were bothering her.

She mentioned her issue to one of the teachers she was friendly with at her daughter's high school. The teacher recommended a life coach she had worked with in the past. Afia made an appointment. She worked with the coach for a year and transitioned from her job as a secretary at a construction firm to one as a legal secretary. She began school to become a paralegal and started a nonprofit to help African immigrants with legal issues.

When she thought back on it later, she was grateful she didn't throw the lunch at her husband, even though she really wanted to. Afia didn't know it at the time, but pausing and finding her breath that Tuesday morning would change the trajectory of her life and help her find her peace without harming the family she loved so dearly.

VIII. Self

Todd W. had his first drink when he was twelve years old. He was first diagnosed with alcoholism at twenty-nine. The years in between were mostly a blur. He nearly drowned while fishing with his buddies in high school. By college, he was binge drinking nearly every night. It seemed so normal. Everyone else was drunk too. It wasn't until he started failing classes and blacking out regularly that he thought maybe something was wrong. He would wake in the morning with bruises and cuts on his knuckles and had no idea where they came from. His buddies would tell him stories about what had happened. Then one day, he saw a video of himself cursing at a girl on campus. The things he said to her were disgusting. He pulled at her skirt and her blouse. He was sick with embarrassment. He couldn't remember any of it. He was sure any normal person would have stopped drinking after that, but he just couldn't give it up.

One day he was driving back from an all-night party by himself. His friends had tried to stop him from driving, but he wouldn't hear it. Driving his Audi back to his apartment, he took a turn way too fast and drove through the glass door of a beloved Mexican restaurant before passing out at the wheel. All he knew of the story was what was told to him later; when he woke up in the hospital, he couldn't remember any of it. He just felt the pain of his busted-up face, hands, neck, and shoulders. He had also fractured a few bones in his legs. He was a mess.

Todd's concerned and terrified parents quickly put him in a drug and alcohol rehab program after his release from the hospital, where he stayed for three months learning about the damage alcohol does to the body and how to enjoy life without the euphoria he experienced from drinking.

When he came out of the program, he transferred to another school to finish his degree in computer science. He and his counselors thought it would be best to have a fresh start. And he did. He maintained his sobriety and met the girl who would become his wife. They married and had two children.

Then, after five years of marriage, he took a drink while he was at a work conference in Hawaii. *It's just one drink*, he thought, but now he was back to drinking every week—sometimes every day. He enjoyed it and it relaxed him, but everyone he knew complained about his drinking. He couldn't always remember the source of their complaints. His wife said he was too loud, aggressive, or harsh with her. He embarrassed her in public. His close friends at work expressed their concern. His kids didn't say much; they were too young.

Why can't I just enjoy a drink from time to time like everyone else? he thought. There was alcohol everywhere: at restaurants, parties, and work functions; on television and social media; and in movies. *It's normal, for goodness' sake! Why can't I enjoy it like normal people do?*

Aside from being angry about not being able to drink like other people, Todd was also angry he couldn't stop. He remembered his car accident. He still had scars on his forehead and both legs from it. He didn't want to lose his family, but he also didn't want to give up alcohol again. He loved it. Margaritas, gin and tonic, scotch and soda, and cold beer were all favorites. When he drank, he felt like all his worries disappeared, at least for a moment. Most recently, he started drinking vodka. Nobody seemed able to smell it on him. He kept small bottles in his office and in the drawer with his ties.

Holly, his wife, had been after him for a while to fix a leak in the bathroom. He promised he would take care of it on Sunday afternoon. He grabbed a beer and his tools and went to work. His morning beer made him feel both calm and hopeless at the same time.

"Honey, I'm so happy to see you working on the leak," Holly began.

"Yup."

"You know it's only ten in the morning, right?"

"Yup."

"Todd, you are drinking a beer."

Todd could feel the shame rise in the pit of his stomach. He felt like an idiot. He knew he shouldn't be drinking first thing in the morning. It made no sense. But it was as if his body was calling for it. He said nothing. He felt like a fraud. Every day he went around pretending everything was fine, when deep in his soul he knew he was a mess. He was disappointing the people he cared about the most.

His first thought was to make a joke: *It's five o'clock somewhere!* His second thought was to tell her to leave him alone. Instead, he took a breath. Then another. And another.

Holly looked at him with a mixture of annoyance and concern.

Todd looked into his beer can. He couldn't bear to see his wife's face. "I think I need some help."

"Todd, that's good. That's music to my ears."

By letting go of his anger and denial, Todd found an Alcoholics Anonymous meeting in his community and was able to regain his sobriety. He learned to enjoy his life without alcohol and maintain his employment and the love and respect of his family.

BREATHWORK TECHNIQUES TO TRY

The simple stories in the previous section illustrate the power of pausing to take a breath in virtually any situation. While cleansing breaths are an easy way to practice pranayama, there are a number of other ways to include breathwork into your daily routine to improve your overall physical and mental health. Any of these can be used to pause and access the healing power of your breath to avoid making a poor decision based in anger. Using these techniques allows you create space between yourself and your feeling of anger rather than following the feeling, which will inevitably lead you down the wrong path. Below are a few techniques you can try, including a refresher on cleansing breaths.

Cleansing Breaths

Cleansing breaths is one of the simplest breath work techniques and can be used at any time to calm the nervous system, clear the mind, and release tension from the body. To take cleansing breaths, follow these steps:

1. Sit or stand up straight and bring your awareness to your breath. (If you're at home or in a private place, you can also practice lying flat on your back in bed or on the floor.)
2. Inhale through your nose, letting your belly fill up.
3. Exhale through your mouth with an audible sigh. Louder is better, but if you are in a public space even a quiet sigh will help.

Don't you feel better now? Depending on your needs and situation, cleansing breaths can be enjoyed as a single breath or in groups of three or more.

Box Breathing

Box breathing, or square breathing, is another simple technique that you can use to calm your mind and body in nearly any situation. As the name indicates, box breathing involves an equal pattern on four sides. Follow these steps to try box breathing:

1. Sit or stand up straight and bring your awareness to your breath. (If you're at home or in a private space, you can also practice lying flat on your back in bed or on the floor.)
2. Inhale slowly through your nose to a count of four.
3. Pause and hold your breath for a count of four while your lungs are full.
4. Exhale slowly through your nose to a count of four.
5. Pause and hold your breath for a count of four while your lungs are empty.
6. Repeat this cycle: inhaling for four counts, holding for four counts, exhaling for four counts, and holding for four counts. Practice for at least thirty seconds or up to three minutes.

Reiki Breathing

Reiki is an energy healing technique that reduces stress and anxiety and increases relaxation. Through Reiki breathing, you can use this technique on yourself. Follow these steps to practice Reiki breathing:

1. Sit or stand up straight and bring your awareness to your breath. (If you're at home or in a private space, you can also practice lying flat on your back in bed or on the floor.)
2. Rub your hands together until your palms get warm.
3. Place your right hand on your heart and your left hand on your belly.
4. Inhale slowly to a count of three, letting your belly fill. Notice the sensation of the energy of your palms against your body rising with your breath.
5. Exhale slowly to a count of three. Notice the sensation of the energy of your palms against your body falling with your breath.
6. Repeat this cycle: inhaling for three counts and exhaling for three counts. Practice for at least thirty seconds or up to three minutes.

Visualization Breathing

Visualization breathing is a simple technique, but it is not safe to practice everywhere. For example, you shouldn't try this while driving. However, this method is still accessible enough to do in your parked car or in a public bathroom when you need to regroup. While the other breathing methods are designed for stress relief and redirection, visualization breathing will take you even further by allowing you time to focus on a safe space or desired outcome. Follow these steps to practice visualization breathing:

1. Create a mental picture of a safe space or desired outcome.
   - Your *safe space* might be the lake where you loved to go swimming as a child, your grandmother's backyard, or a favorite park in your neighborhood. This works best if the safe space you choose is an outdoor location with some greenery.
   - Your *desired outcome* could be a new job, a life partner, or a beautiful vacation cruise. It should be something that you're working toward.
2. Sit up straight and bring your awareness to your breath. Place your hands on your knees. (If you're at home or in a private space, you can also practice lying flat on your back in bed or on the floor.)
3. Take a few cleansing breaths, inhaling through your nose and exhaling through your mouth, then continue to breathe normally.
4. Hold the image of your safe space or desired outcome in your mind's eye and bring your awareness to your five senses: see, hear, taste, touch, smell. Add a sixth sense: How do you feel in your gut? Using the example of your grandmother's backyard, it may go something like this:
   - *See* grandma's backyard: the grass, trees, swing set, and doghouse. Look around and see the marigolds and honeysuckles, the big porch on the side of the house, and the blue sky.
   - *Hear* the birds chirping in the distance and the rustle of the leaves in the wind.
   - *Taste* the lemonade you just sipped.
   - Notice the *touch* of warmth from the sun against your skin and the coolness of the gentle breeze.
   - *Smell* the honeysuckle, cut grass, and a subtle hint of lemonade.

- Notice how you feel in your *gut*. Your belly feels soft and relaxed. You feel peaceful and happy.
5. Breathe normally as you explore the six senses in your mind, continuing to see, hear, smell, taste, and feel, both against your skin and in your gut.
6. Enjoy the feeling of peace and relaxation you have created with your own mind for up to twenty minutes.

Visualization of a safe space like your grandmother's house or your favorite garden is a great relaxation technique. When you visualize a desired outcome, the impact can be even more profound. According to studies in sports psychology by the National Institutes of Health, mental imagery can increase the likelihood of obtaining desired outcomes by improving self-confidence, managing anxiety, increasing motivation, and improving muscle strength.[3] In his book *Becoming Supernatural*, neuroscience researcher Dr. Joe Dispenza notes that visualization also works to bring forth desired outcomes by aligning your energy with your environment.[4] The brain doesn't know the difference between reality and your imagination. This is apparent during vivid dreams, when you may believe you are in a bar brawl or on a luxury cruise. You can try using visualization breathing whenever you need a break from negative emotions and incorporate it into your daily or weekly routine.

Alternate Nostril Breathing

Alternate nostril breathing is a yogic pranayama practice that brings unique attention to the left and right side of the body. You may find this focus on right and left brings more clarity and balance. While this method is very accessible in just about any situation, it is a bit more complex and is recommended after you have already tried the previous methods outlined above. Because you breathe out of one nostril at a time, you may want to blow your nose before practicing to make sure both nostrils are clear, and since you will be placing your hands on your face and nose, make sure to wash your hands before starting. If you suffer from asthma or any heart or lung condition, pay careful attention to how you feel during this practice. If you feel any light-headedness, shortness of breath, or other discomfort, stop the practice and return to your normal breathing. Follow these steps to practice alternate nostril breathing:

1. Sit up straight and bring your awareness to your breath. (If you are at home or in a private space, you can also practice lying flat on your back in bed or on the floor.)
2. Take three cleansing breaths, inhaling deeply through the nose and exhaling through the mouth.
3. Rest your index and middle finger of your right hand gently at the space between your eyebrows.
4. Rest your thumb lightly on your right nostril and your ring finger on your left nostril.
5. Use your thumb to close your right nostril and inhale through the left nostril.
6. Now switch, releasing the right nostril and using your ring finger to close your left nostril. Exhale through the right nostril. Inhale through the right nostril. Switch.
7. Exhale, inhale, switch.
8. Continue this pattern, exhaling through one nostril, inhaling through the same nostril, and switching your hand position. Practice for at least thirty seconds or up to three minutes.

* * *

Your breath is one of the most powerful weapons in your arsenal to combat the uselessness of anger. You can use simple breathing techniques in the middle of a stressful situation and incorporate daily practice into your routine to manage stress and triggers before they arise. Not only will you benefit from decreasing anger and its negative impact on mental and physical health, but breathwork techniques come with their own benefits that enhance both mental and physical wellness. Enjoy this new way of understanding something you were doing twenty thousand times a day without even thinking about it. Tapping into the healing power of your breath is a huge accomplishment on your journey to clear your life of anger.

KEY POINTS

1. The second step in the five-step Tame and Reframe technique for transforming anger is **Notice Your Breath**.
2. There is tremendous power in learning to use your breath to calm down and refocus with one of many breathwork techniques, for several reasons:
   - Deep breathing gives you something to do.
   - Breathing brings oxygen to the brain.
   - Deep breaths calm your nervous system.
3. Using simple breathing techniques can quickly and significantly improve outcomes in a wide variety of scenarios. Simple cleansing breaths are the easiest technique and can be used anywhere, without exception. Box breathing is another simple technique that can be done even while driving. Other techniques, like Reiki breathing, visualization breathing, and alternate nostril breathing, are best used in a more relaxed environment at work or at home. These techniques can calm anger and improve overall health.

Because humans breathe about twenty thousand times per day, you have twenty thousand opportunities to calm down, focus, and reconnect with your life energy, which in yogic philosophy is called prana. Learning to notice your breath and practice pranayama, or breathwork, will not only lead you on the path toward an anger-free life, it will allow you to slow down and notice all the little things you might be missing. You will learn to stop and smell the roses, notice the sunset, and marvel at the blue jays. If you practice breathwork every day, it will be an easy habit to employ when you are in a difficult situation.

ANGER MYTHBUSTER EXERCISE

Process

1. Grab your journal or electronic device for note-taking.
2. Practice at least one of the breathing techniques you learned in this chapter for one minute. You might find it helpful to use a stopwatch on your smartphone or some other method to track the time.

Feel free to try more than one or even choose a favorite. Make a note of how you feel after trying each technique in your journal.
- Cleansing breaths
- Box breathing
- Reiki breathing
- Visualization breathing
- Alternate nostril breathing

3. Write your answers to the following questions:
   - Which of the stories resonated the most with you? What did they remind you of in your own life?
   - How did those situations play out? What might you have done differently to have achieved a better outcome?
   - Which of the breathing techniques can you commit to practicing daily? When will you practice? In the morning? On the way to work? At bedtime?
   - Describe the last time you expressed your anger. What was the underlying emotion (hurt, fear, embarrassment, etc.)? What was the result?

Practice

- Notice when feelings of anger and its Cranky Cousins arise. When they do, first acknowledge your anger without judgment, then try your favorite breathing technique. Three cleansing breaths are usually accessible in most situations. Simply pause to acknowledge your anger, saying, "I notice my anger," then take three deep breaths, in through the nose and out through the mouth.
- When your anger or its Cranky Cousin subsides, how do you feel? Did creating space between your initial anger trigger by using acknowledgement and breath improve your response? A better response typically allows you to spend less time dealing with your feeling of anger so you can get on with doing the things you enjoy doing.
- Can you identify what happened that you didn't like (your trigger)? Can you identify the underlying emotions? Write them down.

Chapter 6

Gear Up Your Imagination

You are breathing, now open your eyes to the truth.

So far you have learned the first two steps in the five-step Tame and Reframe technique for transforming anger: **Acknowledge Your Anger** and **Notice Your Breath**. In this chapter, you will learn the third step: **Gear Up Your Imagination**.

What crosses your mind when you hear words like "creative" or "imagination?" Does it make you think of actors, playwrights, or circus performers? Does it strike you as whimsical or immature? Perhaps it sparks a longing in you for the days of childhood, when you might have built a backyard fort with friends, drawn for hours in a coloring book, or spent long days lost in daydreaming. It might bring your awareness to a *current* desire to pursue a creative hobby, finally launch your side hustle, or sit down and pen your family story.

Creativity and imagination were probably accepted as part of your childhood, but when you became an adult, you were probably encouraged to focus on more "grown-up" things like your career, family, and home. But while it is true that adults have more responsibilities and less time for daydreaming, your imagination is critical in your ability to develop empathy and transform your anger.

SYMPATHY, EMPATHY, OR COMPASSION?

There is often confusion between sympathy, empathy, and compassion. Let's look at the differences. Sympathy is a feeling of sorrow or pity for someone else's situation. For example, you might feel sympathy for someone who is sick with a very rare disease. You see their pain and you feel bad for them. However, the disease is so rare and strange you cannot imagine what it would be like to be afflicted by it. You don't spend much time thinking about it.

Empathy is when you can identify with someone else's suffering. Maybe you have experienced something similar in your own life, or you can at least imagine it in your own life. For example, you might see a child being bullied and immediately develop empathy because you remember having a similar experience when you were a kid.

Compassion happens when a feeling of empathy is combined with a desire for action. In the case of the person with the disease, you might be motivated to send a greeting card, letter, or care package. In the case of the child being bullied, you might intervene. Many people who have seen the suffering of animals in factory farms and slaughterhouses have made the decision to stop consuming meat and other animal products. Feelings of compassion can also exist without action. For example, if you see a news story about starving children, you may not have the resources to help. However, the *desire* to help is the mark of compassion.

When we look at the differences between sympathy, empathy, and compassion, it becomes clear why one's imagination is so important. Imagination is a critical part of both empathy and compassion. But what does this have to do with transforming your anger into something useful? Let's look at the things that make us angry and see how imagination plays a role.

THE POWER OF IMAGINATION IN ACTION

I. Relationships

Micah R. had been dreading the day her daughter, Kendra, would turn thirteen. She and all her mom friends had been worrying about the teenage years from about their kids' tenth birthdays. When her daughter's thirteenth birthday came around, she threw her a party, just as she did every year. But this year wase different. There was so much anxiety.

"Kendra, stop playing with the decorations!" Micah snapped at her daughter, although she wasn't sure why.

"Mom, you're being so weird."

"I'm fine." Micah knew she wasn't fine, but she didn't know of a way to keep her daughter from getting older.

"Well, I hope you're not going to be too weird. Anna said she turned thirteen and all the adults started treating her differently, like she suddenly became a bad kid."

For some reason, those words stuck in Micah's head. She had been so busy worrying about her daughter turning thirteen and all that could mean. Her body was developing, and she would start getting more attention from boys and even men. If she was anything like her mom, she'd be cutting class and smoking in the bathroom. *Ugh!* Micah realized she had been completely focused on her own feelings and wasn't thinking at all about Kendra's.

Those words kept replaying in her mind: "All the adults started treating her differently." Kendra was right. Micah was already treating her differently, and she hadn't even celebrated her birthday yet. As she prepared for the birthday party, she went over those words in her mind. She thought back to her own thirteenth birthday and how it felt to be a teenager for the first time. She remembered her angst, her longing for guidance from a mother who either ignored her, yelled at her, or complained about her. She could never make her mother happy. As she took the time to remember herself as a teenager, she was able to better relate to her daughter. Kendra probably had the same insecurities she had as a young woman. She probably wanted her mother to connect with her, not push her away. In that moment, she made a commitment to stay connected with her daughter as she transitioned from childhood to womanhood. By tapping into her imagination and generating some empathy, she was able to move from a place of annoyance to one of love and understanding.

II. Driving

Helen J. was driving through the busy streets of midtown Manhattan after meeting up with a few friends for dinner after work. There were far more yellow cabs than regular cars on the road, and she did her best to give them room, knowing they often changed lanes unexpectedly and made sudden stops to pick up passengers. Just as she was making a right turn on Broadway, a taxi backed up half the block and ran into the front of her car. She was incensed! *What kind of idiot would do something like that?*

When she got out of her car, the cab driver started yelling in a language she couldn't understand. Helen yelled back. It was his fault anyway!

When the police came to take the report, the cab driver started speaking in English: "My wife is in the hospital. My mother is dying. I wasn't thinking."

Helen was surprised to hear the man admit fault to the police. She calmed down a bit. She had been cursing him out without even knowing what he was saying back to her. She thought about her own mother. She couldn't imagine what it would be like for her if her mother was sick. She didn't even want to think about it.

From that day on, Helen decided to give other drivers some grace. That cab driver was dealing with the death of his mother, and who knew what other people might be dealing with? She remembered that when she was in labor with her daughter, her husband ran at least ten red lights. And one time when she almost missed her exit on the New Jersey Turnpike, she cut across two lanes of traffic. Everyone honked at her that day. She could imagine that other people might have issues, too. They could be sick, stressed, in a rush, or just in need of a bathroom. When she took a little time to think about the different reasons someone's mind might not be on their driving, it calmed her anger.

III. Society

Tiana B. stopped eating meat after having surgery for colon cancer. It was something her doctor recommended, so she decided to give it a try. She joined a vegetarian group on Meetup and started learning more about the health benefits of a vegan lifestyle. In the process, she also learned about the cruelty of factory farming and the environmental impact of meat production. She learned that billions of animals are killed in the United States for food each year,[1] and when she learned the term "environmental racism," she was livid. It turns out that the most run-down slaughterhouses and factory farms were usually located in communities where Black and brown people live.[2] As a Black woman herself, she was angry.

As she learned about the conditions on factory farms and watched documentaries on the topic, she found herself feeling sorry for the animals. She had two cats at home, and they were like babies to her. She was glad she had stopped eating animals.

It was harder for her to understand why people would take advantage of people in marginalized and oppressed communities by putting toxic plants and facilities in their neighborhoods, but with additional time and thought, she began to understand. For one thing, wealthy (often white) people didn't want these facilities in their own communities, and they were usually the ones with the decision-making power. One thing she knew was that people tend to take the path of least resistance, and it was probably easier to open these types of facilities in communities where the population was less educated or already marginalized. And since they probably didn't get any pushback, the decision makers just didn't care.

Once Tiana went through the process of using her imagination to think and try to understand the perspective of others, it made it easier for her to make a game plan. First, she needed to decide what she wanted to do. She had already decided to go from vegetarian to vegan so her purchases wouldn't support animal cruelty or some types of environmental racism. She decided to also join an activist organization to spread awareness in her community. If she hadn't paused to think about the motivations of the owners and decision makers at these factory farms and toxic plants, she could have gotten stuck in a spiral of anger and inaction, instead of using her knowledge to take constructive action.

IV. Politics

Miranda Y. had built her career on a major social media platform. She started posting online when she was in high school and grew her social media following to more than one million in less than five years. As a result of her hard work and dedication, she turned what started out as a hobby into a full-time business with a full-time paycheck. Through her work as an influencer, she was able to travel all over the country and meet a slew of celebrities and politicians who want to connect with her audience.

One day she received a notification from the platform provider that leaders in her state wanted to ban the platform. She knew that all the social media platforms gathered user information; she didn't understand why this one in particular was being singled out. She worked with her platform provider to lobby congress and created public service announcements to share with her following.

Miranda had taken some time to think about the issue. She knew that a lot of little kids were on social media and that it probably wasn't very good for them. There were days when she struggled with all the images of the seemingly perfect models she felt she had to compete with. She even noticed some of her friends were suffering from what they called "Snapchat dysmorphia." They refused to post pictures without filters and sometimes seem to forget what they looked like. When they looked in the mirror, they never looked as good as they did with one of those beautiful social media filters. So while she needed to make a living, she could also understand the problem the lawmakers seemed to wanted to solve.

By taking some time to sit down, think, and use her imagination to understand other people's perspectives, Miranda was able to defend her work as an influencer, lobby Congress, and still be a voice for some of the younger viewers who really didn't need access to her content until they were a little older.

V. Losses

Scott M. got his dog, Riley, when he was a freshman in high school. When he graduated from college, he was excited to live in his first apartment with his little beagle. One day when he was at work, his girlfriend accidentally let Riley out. Scott and his girlfriend searched the neighborhood for weeks trying to find him before he got word of a dog that had been hit by a truck a few miles away. He was devastated to learn it was Riley. He found himself getting angry with his girlfriend and becoming more and more resentful. *How could she have let the dog out like that?* After weeks of arguing, Scott broke up with her. He just couldn't forgive her.

Months after their breakup, Scott took the time to imagine if things had been in reverse. *Suppose he had let his girlfriend's dog out accidentally and it got killed?* He realized how upset he would be. He would feel so guilty, even though it was just a mistake. Dogs run away all the time, and Riley had always loved to break out of the house when he could.

Although he never rekindled the romance with his ex-girlfriend, taking time to use his imagination allowed Scott to forgive her and to make peace with his loss.

VI. Choices

Rosetta K. had been a senior project manager at a large company for nearly ten years. With her six-figure income, she was able to save for her retirement, purchase a house, and live a comfortable lifestyle. She loved her job—until her manager retired and was replaced by a new hire who rubbed her the wrong way. She tried to find common ground but ultimately decided to walk away from the job to work for a small start-up company—a decision she kicked herself for every day.

At her new company, she was slowly building her reputation. It was like starting from scratch. And as a start-up, the company just didn't have the structure or the resources of her old firm. She wanted her old job back but didn't know how to make that happen. Every morning when she woke up, she looked in the mirror and reminded herself what a stupid decision she had made.

One day she was listening to a podcast while eating her lunch. The host talked about finding creative solutions to problems. It got Rosetta thinking about the decision that she had made. She had made the best decision that she could with the information she had at the time. If she hadn't left her firm, she would probably still be miserable working for her manager. But she had a good track record at the company, so she thought she could apply for a new job at the firm. She had friends who would let her know about available positions. She had gained new experience working for a start-up, which would look good on her résumé and give her a new perspective she could take back to her old firm or to any other job.

Taking the time to imagine different scenarios helped Rosetta come to terms with the decision she made and open herself up to new opportunities to move forward. It helped her to get unstuck from a cycle of disappointment and frustration.

VII. Life in General

Karine H. had a hard upbringing. Between the ages of five and eighteen, she lived in ten different foster homes. When she aged out of the system, her last foster family offered to let her continue living with them if she got a job and contributed to the household expenses. That didn't work out for very long. Before she knew it, she was arguing constantly with her foster mom. She decided to move into an apartment with some friends.

Nothing seemed to work out for her. She worked as a cook in a fast-food restaurant. It was a terrible job, and her boss treated her like garbage. Her hours were long, and when she came home, her apartment was loud, messy, and infested with roaches. It seemed that no matter what she and her roommates did to get rid of them, they just came back. She loved watching reality shows with rich celebrities living in beautiful mansions. It allowed her to escape her own reality.

Karine paused to think. Being mad all the time didn't change anything. Her life was hard. Both of her parents were addicts. All of her grandparents were dead. She had no siblings. Her boss was miserable. Her guess was that he was struggling, too, just like her. She needed to find a way to change her circumstances. She started listening to audiobooks on how to build wealth. She learned about mindset, side hustles, saving, and investing. Having a little bit of hope put her in a better mood each day at work. Her coworkers and customers started to notice.

After doing a bit of research, Karine decided to start a natural hair care business. She created a social media account for her business and started braiding and twisting her friends' hair on her days off. Soon her following was large enough that she could reduce her hours at the fast-food restaurant. She still had a long way to go, but she could see a little bit of the light at the end of the tunnel now. Taking the time to use her imagination, develop empathy, and do research allowed her to find hope in a difficult situation.

VIII. Self

Edwin B. had been running behind schedule for as long as he could remember. He remembered that when he was growing up, his father was always running late too. He considered it a family affliction, this relationship with time. When he worked at the bank, it seemed he was always getting reprimanded for coming in late, whether it was just two minutes or twenty. Over the years, his tardiness cost him too many jobs to count. He tried reading time management books, setting his alarm clock earlier, and ironing his work clothes the night before. Nothing seemed to work. He was a night owl and loved to stay up late into the night. Unfortunately, when the alarm clock went off in the morning, he would berate himself. *There I go again—no discipline!*

He was constantly trying to fit himself into what he considered a "normal" schedule. Then one day it occurred to him that maybe he wasn't the only person who liked to stay up—and wake up—late. He went online and looked for work that was more flexible and allowed him to set his own hours. He found a lot of options, from truck drivers to tech support. With his experience in customer service, he decided to pursue remote customer service work and found a job that offered the perfect hours.

By tapping into his imagination and looking for more creative ways to approach his night owl habit, Edwin was able to find work that fit his natural tendencies and abilities instead of forcing himself to fit into a work schedule that was uncomfortable for him. Instead of constantly being disappointed with himself, he set himself up for success by choosing a routine that felt natural for him.

* * *

In all the above examples, the ability to tap into imagination helped create a desirable outcome. Imagination allows us to develop empathy and to see options for ourselves that may not be obvious, all of which helps to process feelings of dissatisfaction and anger.

HOW TO BOOST YOUR IMAGINATION

Your imagination is like a muscle. For most people, it is very active in childhood. As adults, we often need specific activities to get our imaginations back into gear. Below are some fun ways to get your imagination going.

Read Books and Listen to Audiobooks

When you watch films and TV, your brain does not have to add much creativity to the story. Typically, information is being fed to you so quickly you only have time to interpret what you are seeing. With reading and listening, it's different. Your imagination is forced to fill in the gaps. You must imagine what a character or scene looks like. This leaves plenty of room to expand your creativity. You don't have to give up watching your shows, but try balancing it with one fiction book or audiobook each month. Many libraries and YouTube channels offer free audiobooks.

Listen to a Variety of News Sources

You might have a favorite news channel, but try switching it up to change your perspective. And make sure it's a news channel with qualified journalists and news standards. Some channels you might try are BBC, Al Jazeera, Democracy Now, NPR, PBS, CNN, and news programs on networks like ABC, CBS, and NBC.

Watch Foreign Films

Access to foreign films has expanded in recent years with the growth of streaming platforms. When you watch films, it is normal to identify with the hero of the story. When you watch foreign films, you will identify with another culture. It's a great way to grow your creativity, build understanding, and increase empathy.

Enjoy Creative Hobbies

If your paid work doesn't offer much opportunity for creativity, develop a hobby or two to exercise your creative muscle. If you're not sure where to begin, take a few moments to reflect on what you enjoyed as a child. Start with one activity and go from there. For example, if you enjoyed coloring as a child, there are plenty of adult coloring books on the market designed specifically for creativity and stress relief. If you enjoyed writing or painting, circle back to those things. If you used to enjoy playing an instrument, pick it back up.

Adulthood is also a great time to explore interests you've never been able to tap into. For example, you might have always wanted to dance or play the drums but didn't have a chance in childhood. Now is a great time to develop those hobbies. If you have limited resources, there is a wealth of free information on platforms like YouTube to learn just about any creative endeavor you are interested in. So jump in and have some fun!

Play Games

Next time you are waiting in line, pull out a crossword puzzle, grab a Sudoku, or work on a Rubik's Cube. Invite your friends over for a game night with the board games and card games you played growing up. Even video games and karaoke can boost creativity and imagination, so go for it!

Try Something New

Visit a new exhibit in your town, drive home from work a different way, try a new cuisine, or travel to a new city. Exploring new environments stimulates your imagination with new information that requires processing. It takes you out of the same old routine and expands your frame of reference.

Learn Meditation and Visualization

In Chapter 5, you learned a variety of breathwork techniques, including visualization breathing. Learning to settle your mind and tap into your imagination through meditation are powerful ways to boost your imagination and creativity.

Try Yoga Nidra

You are probably familiar with traditional yoga. You may have even taken a yoga class and learned how to do a down dog or a sun salutation. Yoga nidra, often referred to as "yogic sleep," is quite the opposite. During a yoga nidra session, you don't move at all. Your instructor will guide you to an experience where your body is "sleeping" while your mind is alert. This practice is known to relieve stress and anxiety, improve sleep, and increase creativity and imagination. You might think of yoga nidra as meditation on steroids, so if you enjoy meditation and visualization, give yoga nidra a try!

KEY POINTS

1. The third step in the five-step Tame and Reframe technique for transforming anger is **Gear Up Your Imagination**.
2. Reigniting your childhood imagination helps you to build empathy for others and yourself, solve problems, and find solutions. Empathy is critical in the process of transforming anger.
3. There is an important distinction between sympathy, empathy, and compassion. Sympathy is a feeling of sorrow or pity for someone else's situation. Empathy is when you can identify with someone else's suffering. Compassion happens when a feeling of empathy is combined with a desire for action.
4. Developing your imagination and creativity can be fun! You can listen to stories, play games, use visualization techniques, try new things like yoga nidra, and open yourself up to new ways to enjoy the world around you.

Developing and expanding creativity and imagination allows you to open your eyes to the perspectives of others. Through a wide variety of films, stories, news, experiences, and thoughts, you will broaden your capacity for sympathy, empathy, and compassion. This enhanced perspective will help you process your emotions when things don't happen the way you want them to and develop more kindness toward yourself and others.

ANGER MYTHBUSTER EXERCISE

Process

1. Grab your journal or electronic device for note-taking.

2. Practice at least one of the breathing techniques you learned in chapter 5 for one minute. Feel free to try more than one or even choose a favorite. Write how you feel after trying each technique.
   • Cleansing breaths
   • Box breathing
   • Reiki breathing
   • Visualization breathing
   • Alternate nostril breathing
3. What strategy for building your imagination is most appealing to you? Choose one that you will commit to practicing this week and write it down in your journal.
   • Read books and listen to audiobooks
   • Listen to a variety of news sources
   • Watch foreign films
   • Enjoy creative hobbies
   • Play games
   • Try something new
   • Learn meditation and visualization
   • Try yoga nidra
4. Write your answers to the following questions in a notebook or journal:
   • Which of the stories resonated the most with you? What did they remind you of in your own life?
   • How did those situations play out? What might you have done differently to have achieved a better outcome?
   • Describe the last time you expressed your anger. What was the underlying emotion (hurt, fear, embarrassment, etc.)? What was the result?

Practice:

• Which of the techniques to build imagination do you want to do on a weekly or monthly basis? Write your commitment for the next three months. Perhaps try one item from each category.

Chapter 7

Entertain, Educate, and Enlighten Yourself

You found some space; what will you fill it with?

How's your life? Are you walking in your passion and purpose, or is something holding you back? In Chapter 6, you learned all about the importance of growing your imagination. Now that you've had some practice tapping into your creativity, you are ready for the fourth step in the five-step Tame and Reframe approach to transforming anger: **The Three E's: Entertain, Educate, and Enlighten Yourself.** The three E's will create thoughtful, constructive action, rather than the always destructive action that arises from anger. So far you have learned to **Acknowledge Your Anger, Notice Your Breath,** and **Gear Up Your Imagination.** In this chapter, you will learn what to do with that anger when it arises. Over time you can learn to pivot from moments of anger so quickly they will be barely discernable, if at all. This doesn't mean you'll become a pushover and accomplish nothing in life; on the contrary, you will learn to take powerful action while maintaining your cool.

While previous chapters have explored stories of regular, everyday people, here you can use your imagination and dream big with stories from successful entrepreneurs who have taken everyday annoyances and translated them into successful businesses. An entrepreneurial journey may not be a dream of yours; however, these compelling stories will both entertain and inspire you to take constructive action when faced with adversity or discontent. Remember, before they were icons, they were everyday people, too. While these stories don't speak to the temperament of the entrepreneurs, they exemplify taking constructive action using the three E's. It's never too late to become the focused, productive, passionate, and peaceful person you want to be.

Whether you experience outright, undeniable anger or its 7 Cranky Cousins—disappointment, annoyance, frustration, jealousy, impatience, guilt, and resentment—they *all* can be processed using the five-step Tame and Reframe technique to give you the desired results of either peace or constructive action. The way we get there is by accessing the Three E's: entertaining, educating, and enlightening ourselves as necessary and appropriate.

IN SIMPLE SITUATIONS—ENTERTAIN YOURSELF

There are many small, daily annoyances that can set off a cycle of grumbling and complaints. You might be stuck in traffic, waiting in a long line at the grocery store, dealing with an insensitive remark from a family member, or trying to find your car in the parking lot. Not all anger triggers are worthy of your time and attention. They may not be serious enough for you to put in the effort to get educated on an issue or seek some higher understanding or enlightenment. You may just need a temporary distraction. This is when you should entertain yourself.

If you are stuck in traffic, you might turn on the music in your vehicle, grab a snack, listen to a podcast or audiobook, or call a friend for engaging conversation. If you are waiting in a long line at the grocery store, the simple solution might be to pick up one of the many magazines available and read an article, make small talk with someone in line with you, or google a recipe for dinner. If a family member makes an insensitive remark, you might offer the person grace and not respond negatively and instead turn on the television, do a crossword puzzle, play a video game, or putter in the garden. If you've lost your car in the parking lot, you might call a friend to keep you company and laugh about it while you try to find your car.

Remember, anger doesn't benefit you. It should be transformed as quickly as possible into either peace or constructive action by first acknowledging your anger, then noticing your breath, then gearing up your imagination. Use your imagination to find entertainment when it is an appropriate solution.

WITH MORE COMPLEX ISSUES—
EDUCATE YOURSELF

What annoys you? Perhaps you are vegan and have found it hard to find a good burger and fries, or you've just been feeling undervalued at work. In an earlier time, you might have been annoyed by hair products that don't work, having to carry music and books around, or worryng about your underwear showing through your clothes. Those things probably don't bother you now, because thoughtful inventors turned *their* annoyances into action using imagination and creativity, which is the mark of innovation. Let's look at how some entrepreneurs built empires on their ability to transform annoyance into masterful change by getting educated and taking powerful, lucrative, constructive action.

From Oppressed to Success: Madam C. J. Walker

Madam C. J. Walker, born Sarah Breedlove, was the first self-made female millionaire in the United States. She was the first in her family born after the Emancipation Proclamation of 1863, born on the same cotton plantation where her parents had been enslaved. She worked for more than a decade as a poorly paid washerwoman, one of the few jobs available to Black women at that time. After moving to Denver in 1905, she worked as a cook in the home of a pharmacist and learned the chemistry necessary to create an ointment that healed common scalp ailments that led to hair loss. She was widowed at the age of twenty and was left with a baby to raise. After marrying her second husband, Charles Joseph Walker, she took the name Madam C. J. Walker and began achieving success with her hair products.

Madam C. J. Walker went on to become not only a millionaire but a philanthropist, notably donating $1,000 to the YMCA and $5,000 to the NAACP. At its height, her business employed twenty-five thousand sales representatives.[1] Her story is told by her granddaughter A'Lelia Bundles in the book *Self Made* and was also the subject of a Netflix miniseries of the same name.

Imagine you were born to enslaved people who were forced to endure the highest levels of abuse and degradation in society: denied basic education, chained by the neck, sold at auction, beaten and whipped, hung from trees, bred, raped, and brutalized with no legal protections.

You were also born a woman in 1867, a time when even white women couldn't vote. (The Nineteenth Amendment, guaranteeing all women in the United States the right to vote, wasn't passed until 1920.) Now that you have practiced using your imagination and developing empathy, pause to think about that. How would it feel to have someone legally own you and your children? What would you do if you knew that if you made any wrong move, your children could be sold? How would you respond if the last person who tried to escape for freedom had his feet cut off or was beaten or raped publicly?

While Sarah Breedlove was not born into slavery, her parents were. How would you feel if you were born to formerly enslaved parents? Would you be angry? Annoyed? Resentful? There's no way to know the emotions with which young Sarah Breedlove grappled. It would be safe to assume they ran the full gamut of human responses. What we do know is that she was able to identify something that was missing from her life and sought to create a solution, not just for herself but for millions of other women.

Instead of giving in to the perceived hopelessness of her situation, Madam C. J. Walker was determined to craft a better life for herself and her children. She got creative and took constructive actions. Through her actions she was able to change not only her own circumstances and social status but also those of her family, her business associates, and the thousands of women who worked for her. She uplifted her community with her charitable contributions. She inspired generations of women to believe that they could succeed no matter their circumstances.

From Rejected to Selected: Steve Jobs

The name Steve Jobs is widely known all around the world; he was the cofounder of Apple. Jobs was adopted as an infant and raised in a middle-class family in Cupertino, California. His biological parents were of German and Syrian descent. Disillusionied by the educational system, he dropped out of college after only six months at the age of eighteen and landed a job working for Atari as a video game developer. He saved his money to travel to India for his own personal development and spiritual journey. He ended his trip after developing lice, scabies, and dysentery, then nearly being attacked by a mob after complaining about being sold watered-down milk. However, the trip had a profound impact on him.[2]

When he returned to California, he reconnected with his high school friend Steve Wozniak. When a computer designed by Wozniak was turned down by his employer, Hewlett-Packard, in 1976, the two friends founded Apple. In 1985, when was removed from the board of directors of the company at the encouragement of a CEO he had hired, he quickly pivoted and started a new company, NeXT, which designed powerful computers for the education market. In 1986, he obtained a controlling interest in the Hollywood production company Pixar. Over the next decade, Jobs grew Pixar into a major animation studio that produced the first completely computer-animated feature-length film, *Toy Story*, in 1995. He sold Pixar to Disney in 2006.[3]

When Apple was in trouble in 1996, the new CEO, Gilbert Amelio, purchased NeXT for more than $400 million and brought Jobs back to Apple as a consultant. A year later he was the company's CEO, and the rest is history. Under Jobs's leadership, Apple went on to change the world with revolutionary innovations like iTunes, the iPod, the iPhone, and the iPad.

There are so many moments in the story of Steve Jobs where he could have given in to anger. Even under the very best of circumstances, being adopted can be difficult. College wasn't what he expected. His spiritual pilgrimage was a bit of a bust. And he got kicked out of the company he started. But instead, he redirected his energy to the next positive action: building a new business, designing new products, being a visionary. As of this writing, Apple employs more than one hundred thousand people globally and is credited with making computer technology more accessible for people around the world. This technology has impacted access to education, entertainment, information, and communication across the planet. By taking constructive action, Jobs made it possible for us to put our entire collection of music and books—along with limitless other information—in our back pockets. Now that is revolutionary. And Jobs has inspired innumerable people to think outside the box and pursue their goals even if they don't have a traditional education.

From Bulging to Billionaire: Sara Blakely

In 2012, Sara Blakely, the founder of Spanx, became the youngest self-made female billionaire in the United States. That's billionaire with a "B." Blakely was working as a salesperson at an office supply company and wanted an appropriate undergarment to wear under her white pants. She cut the feet out of her pantyhose and decided it was the perfect solution. She could wear open-toed sandals and still have the slimming effect of the pantyhose. The only problem was that the pantyhose wouldn't stop rolling up. An idea was born. In 2000, she used $5,000 from her savings to research, patent, trademark, produce, and market her footless hosiery. That same year, she got the kind of marketing a new business could only dream of: Oprah Winfrey endorsed Spanx on her show, saying she wore them herself. Blakely's sales skyrocketed.

In 2004, Blakely appeared on the reality show *Rebel Billionaire*, winning the $750,000 prize for second place. She used that money to seed the Spanx by Sara Blakely Foundation, which provides grants and scholarships to woman entrepreneurs.[4] Since its inception in 2006, the foundation has donated millions to charities that empower women and girls across the globe. In 2013, Blakely signed the Giving Pledge, a campaign founded by Warren Buffett and Bill and Melinda Gates, promising to give at least half her wealth to charity. She was the first self-made female billionaire to do so.[5]

Blakely's story sounds like one of many American entrepreneurial journeys, with one big exception: She is a woman. According to 2018 data from the US Census Bureau, less than 20 percent of companies in the United States are owned by women. On average, women-owned firms earn half the revenue of male-owned firms: $1.6 million versus $3.2 million.[6] However, this number can be misleading. According to *Forbes*, only 1.7 percent of all women-owned firms generated more than $1 million in 2018.[7] Part of the disparity may be due to lack of access to funding; while 40 percent of US businesses are owned by women, they receive only 7 percent of venture capital.[8]

With statistics like that, it would have been easy for Blakely to give up. However, she was driven by her desire to help women and create a product that would make them feel good.[9] She could have just written letters complaining to hosiery manufacturers to express her dissatisfaction with their products. Instead, she focused on her vision and created a product that has allowed her to achieve wealth and power while making a significant difference in the lives of women around the world.

From Food Truck to Fortunes: Aisha "Pinky" Cole

Aisha "Pinky" Cole is the founder of the Slutty Vegan restaurant chain and food business, which is valued at $100 million as of 2023.[10] Cole's story is one of ambition, grit, and sheer determination. She was born in Baltimore, Maryland, to Jamaican immigrant parents. On the day of her birth, her father was sentenced to life in prison and was eventually deported to Jamaica after serving more than twenty years. Her mother held multiple jobs to keep the family afloat, and Cole learned about business through prison calls with her father. In 2014, after finishing college, she opened a Jamaican restaurant in Harlem called Pinky's. She lost it to a grease fire in 2016 and "went broke," according to a 2019 interview in *Forbes*. Just two years later, the first Slutty Vegan restaurant opened in Atlanta's historically Black West End neighborhood. Cole wanted to provide easier access to vegan junk food. She started with an Instagram account following and food deliveries, then a food truck, and finally the launch of her first Slutty Vegan location.[11]

Cole was raised by a mother who subscribed to the Rastafarian lifestyle and ate a mostly vegetarian diet. When she was in college at Clark Atlanta University, Cole made the commitment to full vegetarianism.[12] Her Slutty Vegan brand is more in alignment with her values than the Jamaican restaurant she owned earlier, which served meat.

She started her business from her two-bedroom apartment in July 2018, selling her burgers on Instagram. In a few weeks, she was filling orders all around Atlanta and serving burgers from a food truck. When she opened the first Slutty Vegan restaurant in October 2018, just three months later, a crowd of twelve hundred people stood outside in 45-degree weather awaiting the grand opening.[13] It was a marketing masterpiece, and Pinky Cole became an instant sensation.

With its provocative name and equally suggestive menu items, smart marketing, and A-list celebrity endorsements—first Snoop Dogg and then Jermaine Dupri—her business exploded.[14] As of this writing, Slutty Vegan has grown to ten locations, including iconic real estate like Truist Park in Atlanta (home of the Atlanta Braves), Fulton Street in Brooklyn, and the campus of the Georgia Institute of Technology. Her business came full circle when she opened a location in Harlem, just ten blocks away from where her Pinky's restaurant one stood.[15]

Pinky Cole overcame a lot in her childhood: being raised by a working single mom while her father was in prison, with three other siblings who needed attention. She picked herself back up after her first restaurant went up in smoke. She turned her annoyance with the lack of vegan junk food options available to her into a multimillion-dollar business. She could have simply complained or written to one of the big burger chains asking for vegan options—which still would have been constructive action. But she took it to the next level and made big waves in the restaurant business, solved the vegan junk food problem for herself and others, and raised awareness of the health, environmental, and humanitarian benefits of a vegan lifestyle. And she did it all while being not just a woman, but also a Black woman.

The data for Black woman–owned businesses are more discouraging than those for white women. According to 2020 data from the Pew Research Center, while African Americans make up approximately 12 percent of the population, they account for only 3 percent of small business ownership and 1 percent of revenues. Only 37 percent of Black-owned businesses were owned exclusively by Black women.[16]

With these numbers, it would have been easy for Cole to give up before she even started, but she was driven by her desire to bring plant-based foods into historically Black communities. With an infusion of $25 million in funding in 2022 and a business valuation of $100 million, the sky's the limit for this entrepreneur. Food lovers didn't know they needed to be "sluttified" with delicious sandwiches until Pinky Cole came on the scene. Now they can't get enough. She created a business that offers healthier options and lots of fun to communities across the United States, and she is just getting started.

From Student Loans to
Shmillionaire: Rachel Rodgers

Rachel Rodgers is the founder and CEO of Hello Seven, a multimillion-dollar company specializing in business, marketing, financial, and legal training for women, minorities, and other marginalized people. According to the Hello Seven website, only 6 percent of women earn six figures annually, compared to 13 percent of men. Women are

35 percent more likely than men to live in poverty, especially in their later years. In addition, the average net worth of white households is ten times that of Black households. Hello Seven's mission is to even the scales and create more underrepresented and female millionaires.[17]

Rodgers came from humble beginnings. In her bestselling book *We Should All Be Millionaires: A Woman's Guide to Earning More, Building Wealth, and Gaining Economic Power*, she describes growing up poor in New York City and her embarrassment at having to use food stamps. She worried that her friends would find out her family received public assistance. While she spent her early years in a two-parent household, her father passed away when she was in the seventh grade, which contributed to her despairing mother's alcohol addiction. After finishing law school in 2009, Rodgers began her career as a law clerk for a state judge, making $41,000 per year. Just one year later, she launched her own virtual law firm from the comfort of her home and grew it to $700,000 in annual revenue in three years. Many of her clients asked how she grew such a successful business, so she started teaching her strategies. Eventually, the demand for her business coaching was so great that she closed her law practice to coach full time. From there, she began to focus on coaching women to become entrepreneurs, manage their assets, and turn their intellectual property into a seven-figure business. Hello Seven was officially born in 2018.[18]

In 2020, amid the pandemic, the murder of George Floyd, and the rise of social justice activism in the United States and around the world, Rodgers launched the Anti-Racist Small Business Pledge to help small businesses express a long-term commitment to ending racism and promoting racial equity in their organizations. In June of the same year, she had her first million-dollar month, and she hasn't looked back. Hello Seven is currently valued at upward of $12 million. She refers to the members of her coaching membership platform as "shmillionaires," or "shmillies" for short.

Rodgers's message of economic power and inclusivity doesn't stop with her for-profit work. As a mother herself, she created the Hello Seven Foundation to provide resources to Black birthing people in need through vouchers for doulas, night nurses, midwives, and childcare. The inclusive language and messaging of her foundation welcomes diverse populations, including disabled people, immigrant populations, and members of the LGBTQ+ community.

Rodgers could have given up when her father died, when her mother struggled with alcohol, or when she saw her that her $41,000 paycheck might never cover her student loan debt. She could have given in to self-doubt, annoyance, or complacency. Instead, she created one of the first virtual law practices with nothing more than an old Blackberry, a laptop, and $300.[19] When she became a millionaire, she made it her mission to teach other people how to become millionaires too, often using the story of Madam C. J. Walker as an example of prevailing against all odds. It's as if Madam Walker passed the baton on a long throw and Rachel Rodgers grabbed it and threw it forward into her community and beyond.

Learn from These Entrepreneurs—Get Educated

You might be thinking, *I'm not an entrepreneur. I have a regular job and I need to keep it.* That may be true. However, there is a great deal you can learn from these remarkable stories. Entrepreneurship isn't what it was even twenty years ago. With the advent of advanced technologies, many would-be entrepreneurs start with side hustles, including digital products and social media channels that they learn to monetize. The five entrepreneurs outlined here have one thing in common: They saw something they didn't like, and they decided to change it. They all benefited exponentially financially, and the world also benefited from their contributions. They all used one of the Three E's in the fourth step of the Tame and Reframe method: Education.

Each of these successful entrepreneurs saw something they didn't like and set off on a mission to learn what they needed to do to change it. They educated themselves on the problem and created a plan to fix it.

The next time you find yourself angry or annoyed about something substantial, think about these entrepreneurs. What can you do to get educated on a situation that makes you annoyed or angry? How can you bring about constructive action in a meaningful way? It doesn't have to be by building a big company; it might be by starting a church group, a support group for parents, or a book club. If you are annoyed with immigrants, trans people, Black people, or other marginalized communities, your action might be to get educated about those communities by following thought leaders, listening to podcasts, and reading books written by people from those communities. You can find recommended websites in the resources section at the end of the book, and techniques for research and critical thinking are available in the appendix. You can watch diverse news programming presented by people who don't look like you.

Now that you've worked on gearing up your imagination, the sky is the limit. When presented with a problem, don't look to other people for a solution. Tap into your creativity, get educated, and take constructive action.

WITH LIFE'S MOST DIFFICULT ISSUES—ENLIGHTEN YOURSELF

You might find yourself unhappy with deep-rooted and long-standing issues involving your family, the world, or yourself. These types of vast, complicated issues can be overwhelming. You can still choose the path of education to create constructive action, but you may want to go a step further and enlighten yourself. The word "enlighten" describes a spiritual component to your education. By "spiritual," I'm not talking about religion; the two are very different things. While religion is a formal set of beliefs related to the understanding of a supreme power or powers, spirituality is an understanding of yourself as a nonphysical, energetic being and your relationship to the nonphysical, energetic ecosystem or universe around you. This understanding of yourself as a spiritual being may or may not be connected to a formal religion. No matter your belief system, you are a spiritual being and can learn to become enlightened through spiritual understanding.

For example, you might be deeply unhappy with injustice, racism, war, or poverty. You can educate yourself and take action to work for change. However, with large, endemic problems, this may not feel like enough. By enlightening yourself, you can seek education and make worldly changes, but you can also seek to grow spiritually into a wiser, more grounded, and more compassionate person. If you follow a religion that teaches you to hate or harm other people, it's not a spiritual practice; it's false teaching and it will lead you into spiritual trouble. It may even get you into legal trouble. When in doubt, follow empathy. You've practiced it enough to have a good handle on it.

Enlightening yourself doesn't cause harm to you or other people. It's a constructive action that causes positive change within yourself. Some methods of enlightening yourself—like meditating, journaling, and various types of yoga—are described in this book. Another practice is learning to pray, not only for yourself and people that you care about but "for the good of all." The fact is that sometimes things will make you outraged and you may not be able to have the impact you want, even if you started a multimillion-dollar company to fix the problem. Working on your spiritual self is an important part of transforming your anger and maintaining your cool. It's like finding an oasis in the middle of a vast desert.

* * *

The three E's are all about taking action—but not just any action: positive, useful, constructive action. They are about the types of actions that make you proud and build your legacy, not the types of action that cause pain and regret. The faster you can shift from feelings of anger in all its variations to useful, purposeful, good work, the calmer, happier, and more fulfilled you will become.

KEY POINTS

The fourth step in the five-step Tame and Reframe technique for transforming anger is the Three E's: **Entertain, Educate, and Enlighten Yourself**.

1. The Three E's allow us to pivot appropriately to either a sense of calm or necessary, useful, and appropriate action.
2. In simple situations: Entertain Yourself. Not all anger triggers are worthy of your time and attention. Getting stuck in traffic, waiting in line at the grocery store, dealing with an insensitive remark, or losing your car in the parking lot are all good examples. They may not be serious enough for you to put in the effort to get educated on an issue or seek any type of higher understanding or enlightenment. You may just need a temporary distraction. Do something fun like listening to a podcast or calling a friend.

3. With more complex issues: Educate Yourself. Find ways to get educated on larger issues. Look for ways to take action. Be inspired by stories of entrepreneurs who found a problem and created a solution. You may not want to be a business owner, but you might want to start or join a support group, church group, or a book club. If you find yourself upset with marginalized communities like immigrants, trans people, or Black people, a good action is to get educated on those communities by reading books and listening to podcasts and other content created by people from those communities.
4. With life's most difficult issues: Enlighten Yourself. When dealing with deep-rooted and long-standing issues, you may feel overwhelmed. You can still choose the path of education to create constructive action, but you may want to go a step further and enlighten yourself by embarking on a spiritual path to understand the connection between your nonphysical, energetic self and the nonphysical, energetic ecosystem or universe around you.

Learning to pivot to actions that feel good to you and others around you is one of the most important aspects of transforming your anger and negative energy. The faster you implement the Three E's in your life, the sooner you can enjoy a more joyful and fulfilled life.

ANGER MYTHBUSTER EXERCISE

Process

1. Grab your journal or electronic device for note-taking.
2. Practice at least one of the breathing techniques you learned in chapter 5 for one minute. Feel free to try more than one or even choose a favorite. Write how you feel after trying each technique.
3. Write down your answers to the following questions:
   • What simple situations do you find upsetting? Have you ever tried to entertain yourself to distract yourself from a triggering situation? How did it turn out? What ideas can you create now to entertain yourself if a simple anger trigger like traffic interrupts you in the future? Write down at least three ideas.

- Which of the entrepreneur stories resonated with you the most? Why? What ideas can you think of and get educated about to solve personal pet peeves or things that really annoy you?
- What struggles are so deeply rooted, long-standing, and overwhelming for you that dealing with them will require some enlightenment? Which techniques for enlightenment do you currently use? Which ones would you like to explore?

Practice

- Over the next few days, try entertaining yourself when faced with small annoyances.
- Identify larger issues that make you annoyed and create a plan for positive action. It can be a simple plan or small action. Use your imagination.
- Practice a daily or weekly spiritual routine that nourishes you. It could be a few minutes of prayer, yoga, journaling, breathwork, meditation, or even a quiet walk in nature. Use your imagination. What makes you feel good and connected to your spiritual self?
- Write in your journal how it feels to have all these options and solutions for dealing with things that might have made you feel helpless before.

Chapter 8

Recognize Your Success

Give yourself permission to celebrate yourself.

When was the last time you stopped to celebrate your accomplishments? Even the small ones? Since you have gotten this far, the hard work is done. You have learned the first four steps in the five-step Tame and Reframe approach to transforming your anger. You know how to **Acknowledge Your Anger, Notice Your Breath, Gear Up Your Imagination**, and use The Three E's to **Entertain, Educate, and Enlighten Yourself,** depending on what is most appropriate for you at the time. In this chapter, you will learn the final step: **Recognize Your Success.**

You can recognize your success in small ways or large. I recommend you get in the habit of recognizing every time you don't rise to your anger, even if it's just one second of self-acknowledgement. While this step may seem inconsequential because it is so simple, it's important not to skip it. Positive reinforcement is critical in creating new habits. When you first find yourself working with the five-step Tame and Reframe technique, you might find yourself counting out the steps in your head.

Of course, you don't want to go through the rest of your life counting out steps. That's why the fifth step is so important. Recognizing your own success and creating a good feeling at the end of the process provides the positive reinforcement necessary to make the Tame and Reframe technique a habit. You may have experienced the impact of positive reinforcement when you've tried to change your behavior in the past. For example, when you were a child, you might have gotten a gold star on your homework when you got a good grade. That gold star probably felt good, so you wanted to do what was required to get another one. I used to love getting gold stars, and now in my coaching practice, my clients still love to get certificates of completion and other acknowledgements of their progress and transformation. Our brains are hardwired for acknowledgement; that's why you probably feel miffed if you do something nice for someone and they don't bother to say thank you.

WORK AND REWARD IN HABIT CREATION

Here are some other common examples of the work-and-reward connection in habit creation:

- You are trying to create a habit of walking (or running) for thirty minutes in the morning, so you don't have your coffee until your exercise is complete. In this case, the coffee is the reward.
- You want to get to work earlier in the morning, so you remind yourself that you will avoid traffic and enjoy the drive if you leave earlier. Here, the peaceful drive is the reward.
- You want to lose weight, so you reward yourself with a low-calorie strawberry protein smoothie after each workout. The delicious beverage is the reward.

Now it's time for you to learn how to reward yourself consistently whenever you transform your anger to peace or constructive action. Over time, you will run through the five steps in the Tame and Reframe process so quickly, you won't even realize you did it. That's the ultimate gift: a peaceful, passionate, and productive life. There are two main types of rewards: the reward in the moment and the future reward.

The Present Reward

Each time you successfully work through the Tame and Reframe technique and process your anger, reward yourself right there in the moment. This "present reward" really is a gift to yourself. Here are several ways you can do that:

- **Pause and congratulate yourself with positive self-talk.** You may think to yourself, "Wow! You're getting good at this," "Great job!," or "I feel great and no regrets."
- **Take a moment and say a favorite affirmation.** It could be "I am growing stronger every day," "I am in control of my destiny," or "I am a boss!"
- **Do a quick visualization.** Take a moment to imagine the future you desire using all five senses. Every time you transform your anger into something honest and useful, you are a fraction of a step closer to the life you want.
- **Enjoy a physical display of victory.** If you are alone in your car or some other private or appropriate place, you might want to use your body: It could be a few finger snaps, hand claps, or even a little dance.
- **Smile.** It seems very simple, but if you aren't in the habit of smiling easily, start. Smiling might be the easiest way to improve overall mood. According to behavior change expert Mark Stibich, smiling offers ten major health benefits:
  1. **Smiling reduces stress.** Even if you don't feel happy, smiling can make you feel more relaxed. Don't try to force a fake smile, but even in difficult moments think about what you are grateful for and allow yourself to smile naturally.
  2. **Smiling elevates your mood.** Your smile can trigger the release of feel-good hormones like dopamine and serotonin as well as neuropeptides, which relax your nervous system. Smiling can work like a natural antidepressant.
  3. **Smiling is contagious.** When you smile, you are silently encouraging someone else to experience all the health benefits of smiling.
  4. **Smiling can boost your immune response.** It is believed that because smiling garners the release of neurotransmitters, it helps to keep you well in the face of viruses or other potential infections.
  5. **Smiling can lower blood pressure.** With all the feel-good and relaxation benefits of smiling, it makes sense that it would lower stress-induced high blood pressure.

6. **Smiling reduces pain.** Did you know that both endorphins and serotonin are natural painkillers? So, yes, smiling also reduces aches and pains.

7. **A great smile makes you attractive.** You probably find yourself drawn to people with a smile on their face. Smiles are welcoming and encouraging. They can also make you look youthful—not only because children are more apt to smile and play, but because the muscles you use to smile lift the face, creating a younger appearance. You also can't see laugh lines when you are smiling, so smile away!

8. **Smiling makes you look successful.** Who doesn't want to look like a million bucks? Smiling in a business environment can make you look more confident and competent.

9. **Smiling helps you to be positive.** Smiling sends so many positive signals to the brain and body, it makes you feel good.

10. **Smiling can increase longevity.** With all the other health benefits, it's logical that the overall impact would be increased life span.[1]

Whatever you do to reward yourself in the moment, make sure it's fun and satisfying for you. The more enjoyable it is, the faster you will create the habit of transforming anger into peace or constructive action.

The Future Reward

At the end of each week, take the time to celebrate your accomplishments in reducing the anger in your life. Do your best to use healthy, nonaddictive, self-validating, and self-affirming rewards. These may be unfamiliar to you. You are probably familiar with common rewards like alcohol, sweet or rich food, and even sex. Here are a few ideas for rewards that are difficult to overdo:

- **Plan personal time.** Take a nap, read for pleasure, or enjoy a bubble bath. Set aside some quiet time that's just for you.
- **Take a stroll around the block or a walk in nature.** Stretch your legs and get some fresh air. Whether you are walking around your neighborhood, strolling in the park, or visiting a hiking trail, take some time to enjoy the outdoors.

- **Get a massage.** Massage has many health benefits, including improved circulation, increased relaxation, reduced stress, improved immune system functioning, and decreased pain.[2] You might think of massage as something you'd find at a high-end spa or hotel, but there are many inexpensive and reputable massage centers available. Find one that is right for you and treat yourself. You might even set aside special "spa time" with your partner.
- **Spend time with friends.** Call a friend for bowling, tennis, basketball, roller-skating, a movie, dinner, game night, or whatever you like to do. If you don't have a community of people who are positive and like to engage in healthy behavior, look for groups at your local community center or on Meetup.
- **Take a yoga class.** Yoga can be a wonderful way to celebrate after a long week. Call your local yoga studio or search YouTube videos for a class that seems enjoyable. Keep in mind there are different types of yoga classes. Traditional yoga, typically advertised as vinyasa or hatha, can leave you sweating. Slower yoga classes are yin, or deep stretch; restorative, which is completely relaxed, just like the name sounds; and yoga nidra, or yogic sleep. You might also find chair yoga for people who are older, new to yoga, or have limited mobility. Make sure to practice only what is safe for your body.
- **Take a guided meditation class.** There are many guided meditations available on apps like Calm or Headspace and on YouTube. You can also look for Buddhist centers like Kadampa Meditation Centers, which are located all around the world.
- **Buy yourself a treat.** If shopping and overspending are problems for you, this may not be the right celebration. However, if you are the type of person who has a hard time spending money on yourself, this might be perfect. So buy yourself a new lipstick, shirt, or bouquet of roses. You deserve it!
- **Visit a sauna.** You may have visited a sauna at your local gym or YMCA. Or perhaps you've visited a traditional Korean sauna and spa or another type of sauna center. According to Harvard Medical School, the dry heat in a sauna has a profound effect on the body and is beneficial for heart health in most people. The pulse rate jumps, increasing circulation to the skin. However, sauna is not appropriate for people with uncontrolled high blood pressure or

heart disease.[3] You might also explore infrared saunas. These saunas are different from traditional saunas because they use infrared lamps that use electromagnetic radiation to warm your body directly instead of just warming the air around you. Because of this, infrared saunas don't feel as hot, and you can enjoy them for longer.[4] Whatever you feel about the health benefits, give a sauna a try if it's safe for you to do so. For most people, taking a sauna simply feels good.

- **Go see a movie or show.** If you've never been to a movie alone, give it a try. It's a liberating experience to not have to depend on someone else's schedule or personal preferences and go see a film or show you want to see. If you prefer to bring a friend or partner, go ahead and have fun. However, it is empowering when you learn to entertain yourself whether someone is with you or not.
- **Spend time with animals.** Animal therapy is a legitimate method of treatment for people managing mental health issues like anxiety and stress. While dogs are mostly commonly used, other animals, including cats, birds, pigs, and horses, can also help you feel comforted and supported.[5] Working through a lens of compassion, look for animals in places that don't perpetuate animal abuse. Some great options are animal shelters, rescues, and sanctuaries.
- **Try laughter yoga.** We know smiling is good for you, but what about laughing? While laughter yoga isn't a *true* form of yoga, it is a great way to relieve stress and get a cardiovascular workout. (Laughing is harder than you think.) You can access sessions in person or online at LaughterYoga.org.[6]
- **Take yourself out to lunch (or dinner).** While you don't want to create a habit of eating an unhealthy meal whenever you want to celebrate, taking yourself out for a delicious meal is a real treat. If overeating is an area of concern for you, focus on healthy, balanced, and nutritious meals. Try a vegan restaurant or healthy ethnic options like sushi, Indian, or Mexican foods (without all the meat and cheese).

Use your newly energized imagination and add to this list. Think about what the kindest thing you could do for yourself would be in any given moment. Have compassion for yourself as well as others. When you don't succumb to the temptation of the old anger habit, you *deserve* to be rewarded repeatedly.

THE IMPORTANCE OF SELF-VALIDATION
AND SELF-AFFIRMATION

Taking the time to pause and reward yourself for your own personal development is an important skill for your mental health. Learning to validate and affirm yourself is a powerful component of this final step. Self-validation is defined as "the feeling of having recognized, confirmed, or established one's own worthiness or legitimacy."[7] When you reward your own behavior, you send the message to yourself that you are worthy. Yes, this is about worthiness. You are good enough to not only own your feelings but process them in a healthy and productive way as well. Over time, you will develop the skill of self-validation. You will not depend on someone else to tell you that you are doing the right thing. You will feel it in your heart and in your mind.

You are doing important work in this book. Learning the Anger Myth is a huge benefit to you and everyone in your family and community. However, not all of your friends and family will be able to understand or support you. If you depend on external validation, you will likely fail. Learning to validate yourself will empower you. It will build your confidence so you can take your new calm and productive disposition into any area of your life. Self-validation will allow you to remind yourself of the importance of the work you are doing to improve yourself. It is part of the pause you need to help you process your progress.

Self-affirmation can be defined as "belief in yourself, your worth, and your ability to achieve things."[8] In that way, affirming behavior is more forward-thinking. When we look for validation, it is typically for something that has already happened. When we affirm ourselves, chances are it is for a future event. It's important to do both, and they are connected. When you successfully transform your anger, you can validate yourself by saying to yourself, "Good job!," or giving yourself some other immediate reward. Afterward, you can affirm yourself: "I'm getting good at this. I can do this. I see myself as a happy and peaceful person."

Here are a few more examples of ways to pause and reward yourself in the moment with self-validation and self-affirmation techniques:

Self-Validation	Self-Affirmation
"That was a close call, but I made it!"	Smile and visualize always maintaining your cool.
"I know I'm on the right path."	"I see a calmer, happier me coming into fruition."
"I love going to the movies by myself."	"I have plenty of friends and I enjoy my own company."

As you work through the five-step Tame and Reframe technique, you may be tempted to skip this final step. Many Western cultures glorify movement and activity and overlook the power in pauses, rest, and acknowledgment. Don't buy into that. You must pause to recognize your wins, consistently and repeatedly. By creating a positive outcome every single time you work through the five-step Tame and Reframe approach, you will reinforce the behavior and build your new habit.

POSITIVE REINFORCEMENT
AND BEHAVIOR CHANGE

This idea of using positive reinforcement to change behavior is associated with the work of B. F. Skinner, a behavioral psychologist who conducted groundbreaking work on behavioral conditioning in the 1930s and 1940s. Positive reinforcement refers to providing a desirable stimulus—like a reward—after a behavior. According to Skinner, there are four ways to provide positive reinforcement: natural, social, tangible, and token.[9]

- **Natural reinforcement is part of the action itself.** In the case of transforming anger, your natural reinforcement is the calm, peace, and happiness you enjoy by not rising to anger and its 7 Cranky Cousins: disappointment, annoyance, frustration, jealousy, impatience, guilt, and resentment.
- **Social reinforcers are external.** While you work on transforming your anger, you may experience social reinforcement. Your

family and friends may notice something is different and comment on your improvement. Your boss or customers may do the same. Social reinforcement is nice, but it's also unreliable. That's why it is so important to learn to self-validate and self-affirm.

- **Tangible reinforcers are physical rewards.** While all the rewards suggested as "in the moment" were intangible, like smiling, visualizing, or snapping your fingers, many of the future rewards shown were tangible: buying a lipstick, going to a movie, or visiting a sauna. Healthy and rewarding activities that nourish and encourage you are particularly helpful. They don't take up space in your home and they contribute directly to your personal development.

- **Token reinforcers are nonphysical and can be redeemed for something of value.** You've probably experienced this with the myriad points systems used in frequent flier rewards and other customer loyalty programs. Perhaps in school you had a teacher who used a point system to motivate students. When you pause to reward yourself in the process of learning the five-step Tame and Reframe technique, a token reward system is most aligned with your weekly future rewards. You mentally note your ability to maintain your peace during the week, or if you prefer, you can make a check mark or some other note on your calendar each day. At the end of the week, you reward yourself based on the number of checks or other determination of your "performance." If you choose to create a check or point system, have fun with it. Any method of positive reinforcement will help you achieve your goals.

HOW NEW HABITS ARE BORN

Research from Duke University indicates that habits account for 40 percent of daily behavior.[10] According to James Clear, author of the *New York Times* bestseller *Atomic Habits*, there are five main ways to create a sustainable new habit: start with a very small habit, increase your habit in small ways, break habits into chunks, get back on track quickly when you slip up, and be patient.[11] The goal is to make the five-step Tame and Reframe approach a daily habit for managing triggers and moments of anger. Consider how the strategies outlined by Clear can help you create new behaviors:

1. **Start with something small.** The one small habit to work on—
   and your top priority—is implementing the five-step Tame and
   Reframe approach every time you are presented with a trigger.
   This is a game changer. It is both small and HUGE, with the
   power to have a monumental positive impact on your life. Think
   of it as the single acorn that produces a mighty oak tree. Don't lose
   focus on this one life-changing habit.
2. **Build on your habit in small ways.** Once you have developed a
   sense of ease with the five steps, feel free to add other new behaviors into the mix. You have already tried breathwork, reading, and
   journaling with this book. Chapter 10 will offer even more ways
   to build on your new habit of transforming anger into either peace
   or constructive action.
3. **Break habits into chunks.** The five-step Tame and Reframe
   approach can be simplified when you are just starting. If the five
   steps are difficult for you, start with just one or two: Acknowledge
   Your Anger and Notice Your Breath. When you are comfortable
   with these, perhaps add two more: Gear Up Your Imagination and
   Entertain, Educate, and Enlighten Yourself. When you are ready,
   use all five steps together. It is perfectly acceptable to break the
   five steps into chunks to give yourself time to learn and process
   them—and don't forget to reward yourself for your progress.
4. **If you make a mistake, get back on track quickly.** Offering
   compassion for others, including nonhuman animals, is important.
   It is also critical to offer grace to yourself. We all make mistakes.
   When you find yourself rising to anger and acting in a way you
   might later regret, forgive yourself and try again. Do not waste
   any time berating yourself. Apologize to other people if you need
   to, forgive yourself, and get back on track.
5. **Be patient with yourself.** You may have had an experience in your
   past when you tried to create a new habit and you were unsuccess-
   ful. Perhaps you wanted to work out five days a week, learn a new
   language, or take up a new sport like tennis or roller-skating. With
   any new endeavor, there will be setbacks. Maybe you discovered
   that learning a new skill is hard and you gave up. Incorporating
   the five-step Tame and Reframe approach into your life is far
   more important than learning a recreational activity, even one that
   is healthy. Learning to transform anger will impact virtually every

area of your life. Don't give up. Give yourself time and grace, and you will make the progress you desire.

THE FIVE-STEP TAME AND REFRAME METHOD IN ACTION

There are hundreds of ways the Tame and Reframe approach can show up in daily life. Here are a few common examples:

1. **Someone cuts you off in traffic.** Acknowledge your anger, take a few breaths (being sure to notice them), and gear up your imagination: What might have caused the other driver to cut you off? Have you ever cut someone off when you were lost, rushing, or worried about missing your exit? Next, it's time to entertain yourself: turn up your music, listen to a podcast, or call a friend. Recognize your success with a smile! That could have gone so differently, but because of your new habits, you are still enjoying the car ride.

2. **Your significant other doesn't give you a romantic gift for a special occasion.** It's your birthday and your husband bought you the toaster oven you saw on late-night television. You have told him a million times that you want romantic gifts, and you are feeling frustrated. First, acknowledge that Cranky Cousin. You have the right to feel the way you do. Then, take a few breaths and notice them. Next, gear up your imagination: What could possibly be going on in your husband's mind that makes him want to buy you a toaster? You may have heard that men can be more into electronics; maybe he is providing a gift he would like to receive. Maybe he is just being practical. Either way, it is a gift. Perhaps it's time to get educated on how to take constructive action. You can either accept his gift choices or find another way to get what you want: Suggest he takes you shopping, have your best friend help him shop, or use a wish list to choose your next gift. Wow! You smile and recognize your success by telling yourself, "You got this!" You no longer feel frustrated or resentful. You will happily accept your toaster, knowing it was given with love, and you

have a plan of action to move the needle for next time to receive the type of gift you really want.

3. **You are overlooked for a promotion at work.** You know you deserved that promotion. You are disappointed, annoyed, frustrated, and downright jealous of the coworker who managed to get the position you wanted for yourself. First, acknowledge your feelings. They are all valid. Next, take a few breaths and notice them. Now, gear up your imagination: Is it possible your coworker was the better candidate? Do you know how you were assessed? Did you advocate for yourself? What parts of the situation could you be missing? Clearly, this is a time to get educated and plan for constructive action. Gather the information you need to assess the situation. Should you schedule a meeting with your manager to create a plan to get you on track for the next promotion? Should you schedule a meeting with your coworker to find out any specific efforts they made to land the role? Do you need a mentor or more credentials? Perhaps you should purchase a career book, hire a career coach, or begin assessing the job market. Now pause and recognize your success! Say to yourself, "Look at me over here slaying dragons. I'm a beast!," or, "I can't believe I worked through my feelings so quickly in a positive way!" This doesn't mean you won't still have moments of sadness because you weren't chosen for something you wanted. However, by using the Tame and Reframe technique, you can quickly reframe your angry feelings so you don't damage relationships with other people and even your own self-esteem.

4. **You didn't pass an exam.** It was your second time taking your road test, and you didn't pass again. You are so disappointed and frustrated. How come everyone else can get a driver's license and you can't? You are mad at the examiner and angry with yourself. You feel like such a loser. Take a moment to acknowledge your feelings. Then take a few breaths and notice them. Now, gear up your imagination: You know you are not the only person to ever fail the road test twice. The examiner was just doing her job. This isn't the end of the world; it's more of an inconvenience. You need to educate yourself: What can you do differently to pass next time? You failed because of your parallel parking. Maybe you can hire a driving instructor instead of letting your friends teach

you. That would be an appropriate action to take. You make the commitment to do something different to get different results next time. Now it's time to recognize your success! You could have spent the whole day moping around and complaining, but instead you have a path to move forward. Say to yourself, "I am going to get my license one day and I will be so proud" or "I'm a great person with or without a driver's license." This doesn't mean you can't acknowledge that you didn't get what you wanted. That's life. You are 100 percent guaranteed to not always get what you want. However, you have learned a new technique to help you quickly reframe your negative feelings so that you don't delay your progress or damage your self-worth.

5. **Someone bumps into you and doesn't say "Excuse me" or "Sorry."** Your first inclination is to turn around and drop a couple of F-bombs, but instead you pause and acknowledge that feeling. How dare they? Next, take a moment to take a few breaths and notice them. Now, gear up your imagination: Maybe they are rushing somewhere, someone is sick, or they are just distracted. Perhaps they are having a really terrible day or were just raised with no manners or consideration. Whatever their issue, you are glad you aren't them. Since there's no point engaging with that person, you decide to entertain yourself. You pull up a podcast episode to distract yourself and go on about your day. You pause the podcast for just a moment to recognize what you did. The old you would have gotten into a screaming match—or maybe even a fight—with the person. Tell yourself, "I'm the bigger person for not getting into altercations for no reason" or "I am creating the life I have always wanted." You saved yourself from additional trauma, drama, and headache by avoiding a meaningless confrontation.

6. **You witness a viral video showing police brutality.** You are tired of watching police bodycam footage show young unarmed Black men and boys being killed. It makes your blood boil. Pause and acknowledge your feelings. You have Black sons. You are angry, scared, overwhelmed, and terrified. Now, take a few breaths and notice, then gear up your imagination: What must it feel like to be a white police officer engaging with the Black community? Schools in the United States don't teach any reasonable history

about Black people except slavery, the Civil War, and civil rights—and they barely teach that. That officer is probably woefully undereducated. He believes he is superior and likely also believes Black men have superhuman strength. He shouldn't be doing that kind of work and he should be punished for his actions, but what can you do? You decided to get educated. You can't solve a problem this big by yourself, but you can make sure you are a part of the solution. You decide to reach out to an acquaintance who is a police officer to learn about the training process for officers. That way you can begin to better understand the problem. You also decide to make small monthly donations to the NAACP, ACLU, and Black Lives Matter. You realize you need more and make a commitment to enlighten yourself. You need spiritual support to process this level of pain. You make plans to read a book a friend recommended to you called *How to Solve Our Human Problems* by Geshe Kelsang Gyatso in the evening and go to a yoga class in the morning. You pause and recognize your success. In the past you might have watched the video over and over, getting more and more enraged and feeling more and more hopeless. This time, you watched the video and were able to transform your anger into constructive action. You say to yourself, "I'm so proud that I am taking action on a cause I believe in," "I'm creating a healthy legacy for my sons," and "I'm shoring up my spiritual life." Of course, the video still hurts. It's unconscionable and outrageous, but you have created a way to process your emotions.

Learning to celebrate and recognize your success is an essential component in the Tame and Reframe approach. It closes the positive reinforcement loop and it's fun! Give yourself permission to enjoy a life free from anger and the pain it causes—and be prepared for new levels of joy, inspiration, and fulfillment in your life.

KEY POINTS

1. You now have all five steps in the Tame and Reframe technique for transforming anger. You can easily remember the steps because the spell out the word **ANGER**:

- Acknowledge your anger.
- Notice your breath.
- Gear up your imagination.
- Entertain, educate, and enlighten yourself.
- Recognize your success.

2. Our brains are hardwired for positive reinforcement. It's important to reward yourself when you successfully reframe your anger into a constructive action to help you develop a new habit. It will also make your habit formation more enjoyable.

3. When you Recognize Your Success, you reward yourself in the moment with positive self-talk, a favorite affirmation, a quick visualization, a physical display of victory, a smile, or some other small behaviors.

4. At the end of each week, celebrate your accomplishments in reducing the anger in your life with bigger rewards that are healthy, nonaddictive, self-validating, and self-affirming. Some examples are walking in nature, getting a massage, spending time with encouraging friends, taking a yoga or meditation class, going for a sauna, going to a movie, visiting an animal sanctuary, or buying yourself a treat.

5. It's important to learn to validate and affirm yourself as you work through transforming your anger. Validation is typically for something that has already happened; affirmation is usually for a future event. It's important to do both.

6. Prioritize learning the Tame and Reframe technique and making it a habit, but also make sure to have patience and self-compassion as you work to develop this new skill.

As you practice the Tame and Reframe method, you will be able to run through the five steps more quickly and easily. It will feel good to you because you will always reward yourself. Let your life feel good. By establishing new mental habits, you are laying the foundation for a life that is both calm and passionate, relaxed and exciting, peaceful and productive.

ANGER MYTHBUSTER EXERCISE

Process

1. Grab your journal or electronic device for note-taking.
2. Practice at least one of the breathing techniques you learned in chapter 5 for one minute. Feel free to try more than one or even choose a favorite. Write how you feel after trying each technique.
3. Write a positive affirmation statement that you can use for a present reward. It should be something believable, like, "I am getting better every day," or, "I deserve to live a happy and peaceful life." Write one that resonates with you and your situation.
4. Write down your answers to the following questions:
   • Are you in the habit of rewarding your accomplishments in healthy ways? Why or why not?
   • Which of the six examples of the Tame and Reframe method in action resonated with you most? Why?
   • Write a list of at least three present and three future rewards you will use as you practice the Tame and Reframe approach in your daily life.

Practice

• Over the next few days, try using the full five-step Tame and Reframe technique. If you find it daunting, practice the first few steps until you get in the habit of using all five.
• Decide how you will celebrate for the week and go enjoy yourself. You are doing a great job!

PART THREE

The Side Effects

Chapter 9

Build Empathy as a Happiness Strategy

You can see, now allow yourself to feel.

If someone walked up to you at the grocery store and asked if you were happy, what would you say? In Chapter 6 you learned how empathy can play a role in transforming your anger into either peacefulness or constructive action. In this chapter, you will learn the profound importance of empathy not just to make you calm, but to make you happy. Happiness can be defined as "a state of well-being and contentment: joy."[1] Who doesn't want that? And guess what? Happy people are less angry.

EMPATHY AND ITS RELATIONSHIP TO HAPPINESS

In the last chapter, you learned that empathy is more than just a feeling of pity; it's when you identify with the suffering of someone (or something) else. But what does that have to do with happiness? In fact, a lot! Research has shown that people who are more empathetic are often happier and more content. This is because empathy is an integral part of healthy relationships.[2] Think about it: Do you want your spouse, boss, children, and coworkers to care about your situation and your feelings? Of course you do. Even in the grocery store, if you hold the door open for someone, you probably want the person to say thank you. That would indicate they care about how you feel and want to acknowledge your kind act. You might even be upset if the person doesn't give that courtesy. It's virtually impossible to build healthy relationships without empathy. It's a two-way street. You must learn to give empathy in the same way you want to receive it.

While relationships can be a source of anger, they are also profoundly meaningful. Humans are social creatures. Relationships with family and community have been necessary for survival from prehistoric times all the way up to the present. Around the world throughout history, governments and societies have been crafted to maintain a social construct. Family and community structures are created to support the survival and success of individuals and society as a whole.

Lack of community, connection, support, and friendship is a major barrier to happiness and can easily feed into anger. As of this writing, the United States has had 531 mass shootings in 2023.[3] Have you ever heard a case of a mass shooter who was happy, empathetic, and surrounded by a supportive community of friends? There is a reason the most violent people in any society are often emotionally isolated. Empathy is critical in both transforming anger and in increasing our sense of happiness.

While empathy is important on an individual basis, it can also connect you to the global community. You may not share the same government, but you share the same sun, moon, stars, and ecosystem with everyone on the planet. It may be easy to develop empathy for your neighbor or your children, but can you grow empathy for people in a foreign country who have a culture that is unfamiliar to you? Developing an appreciation for the global community you are a part of can help you to feel more connected with the world instead of just your community, town, or nation.

Having a sense of connection with your community—whether local, national, or international—can help you identify a sense of purpose. This sense of clarity and meaning increases happiness. American psychologist Abraham Maslow is well known for his theory of psychological health based on fulfilling human needs, culminating with self-actualization, or the fulfillment of your highest potential.[4] This is the highest level of happiness and the fulfillment of your highest calling. So you can see that there are many good reasons to build your empathy. It doesn't just benefit other people; it can rock your world!

CAN EMPATHY GO TOO FAR?

For some people, empathy can become dysregulated. You may have heard the term "empath" to describe those who not only feel empathy for others but are unable to disconnect the emotions of others from their own. This can be a problem. Imagine seeing someone in pain and feeling so much pain yourself that you find yourself crying, shaken, and unable to render any assistance. It can also be a problem because it makes it easier for an emotional predator to take advantage of you.

According to clinical psychologist and author Dr. Ramani Durvasula, empaths may feel as if they are taking on the emotional state of another person.[5] They may be more likely to dwell on stories of personal suffering and be victimized by people who use these types of stories to manipulate others, like people with narcissistic personality disorder and other abusers. While "empath" is not a clinical term, it has become a popular term to describe people who display certain types of behaviors. So how do you know if your empathy is healthy or cause for concern? Here are a few guidelines:

1. **Healthy empathy is not painful.** It is characterized by a balanced awareness of your own emotions and the emotions of other people. Unhealthy empathy may lead you to prioritize the needs of other people over your own mental and physical needs. This prioritization is often fueled by a sense of obligation or commitment, rather than more self-aware and joyful motivations like kindness and desire.
2. **Healthy empathy promotes understanding.** You can process, acknowledge, and validate the feelings of others from a place of discernment. Unhealthy empathy may cause you to take on the emotions of others as if they were your own, to the point of becoming anxious, stressed, and overwhelmed.
3. **Healthy empathy has boundaries.** You can understand the experiences of someone else while still prioritizing your own health and well-being. Unhealthy empathy may involve sacrificing your own mental and physical self-care to help someone else.
4. **Healthy empathy promotes good relationships.** Recognizing the challenges and difficulties of other people sets the stage for healthy communication and meaningful relationships. Empathy

must flow in both directions in the relationship. Unhealthy empathy can lead to toxic relationships in which one person gives empathy but receives none; this can lead to codependency,[6] trauma bonding,[7] and emotional manipulation.

Healthy empathy is essential for transforming your anger into something useful. It's also a cornerstone for overall happiness.

CAN YOU MAKE YOURSELF HAPPIER?

You can absolutely make yourself happier. In her book *Happy for No Reason, New York Times* bestselling author Marci Shimoff shares data from positive psychology researchers showing that 50 percent of your happiness comes from your genetics. In other words, you were born with a particular happiness set point. The good news is that only 10 percent comes from circumstances like wealth, relationship status, or career choice. That leaves the profoundly good news that 40 percent of your happiness is determined by the things you do, and those things can be changed with practice.[8]

In my book *12 Steps to Mind-Blowing Happiness*, I teach a path to joy and deep fulfillment based on:

- **Healing**—the process of addressing past trauma and hurt feelings through therapy, coaching, self-help books, and other healing modalities;
- **Spirituality**—the understanding and nourishment of your non-physical energetic body and your connection to a higher power like the universe, God, or holy beings;
- **Connection**—healthy and supportive relationships with friends, family, and community;
- **Self-Love**—awareness of your own desires, values, and physical appearance combined with a tenderness and appreciation for your unique characteristics and emotions;
- **Peacefulness**—the ability to transform anger into something useful;
- **Generosity**—a willingness to share your talents and resources with the world;

- **Healthy Detachment**—the ability to accept change, live in the present (and not the past), and enjoy people and possessions without clinging on tightly in fear;
- **Surrender**—the ability to speak your intentions to your understanding of God or the universe and to have faith;
- **Patience**—the ability to wait without complaining and trust that all things happen in divine timing;
- **Compassion**—the commitment to be as nonharming as possible to yourself and others;
- **Passion**—a commitment to approach your occupation (even if you don't like it) with energy and enthusiasm, and to pursue the work and activities that excite you and are done in service to others; and
- **Freedom**—the ability to feel spacious, in the flow, and joyful despite life's uncertainties.[9]

The path to a more joyful and fulfilling life is available to you when you take the time to invest in your personal growth. By reading and practicing these techniques, you are on the right track.

WHAT ABOUT GRATITUDE?

An important thread that ties the steps listed above together is gratitude. Consciously appreciating your life and all your experiences will enhance your joy. So you say thank you for your healing, spirituality, community, self-love, peace, talents and resources, ability to change, faith, compassion, enthusiasm for work, and the resulting sense of flow and spaciousness in your life. **You say thank you no matter where you are on your journey, even if you are just beginning.**

You may have heard the word "mindfulness" before. It is another word for being conscious and aware in the moment. That's why a great way to practice gratitude is to pause and focus your attention on what you are thankful for. You might do this with a prayer, meditation, journaling exercise, or even what I call a "Gratitude Shower." This is a way to practice mindfulness and gratitude during your normal shower routine. It's simple: When you are in the shower, instead of thinking about the day ahead, bring your awareness to your physical body and say thank you for the functioning of each body part, both seen and unseen. It might go something like this:

- As you wash your face: "I'm grateful that I can see, smell, smile, and digest my food."
- As you wash your hair: "I'm glad I have a healthy mind."
- As you wash your arms: "I'm so thankful I have healthy arms to carry my groceries and hug the people I love."
- As you wash your chest and belly: "I'm so glad I have a healthy heart, lungs, and digestive system."
- As you wash your legs and feet: "I'm so grateful to have working legs and feet that take me wherever I want to go."
- And when you close you might say: "I realize not everyone has a healthy, functioning body like I do. I am so grateful."

Of course, you may have some issues with parts of your body, particularly if you are a person with a disability. Or you may not like a particular physical feature of your body. If that's the case, taking a gratitude shower at least once a week will have even more of an impact, allowing you to appreciate and make peace with the physical parts of yourself that are most difficult.

MORE TIPS TO BOOST YOUR HAPPINESS

Improving your overall sense of happiness and well-being will make it easier to transform your anger into peace or constructive action. It also feels good. The more we feel good, the less vulnerable we are to negative emotions.

Focus on Solutions Instead of Blaming Other People or Yourself

You may recognize self-blame or shame as one of anger's 7 Cranky Cousins: guilt. No matter what you call it, the tendency to assign blame—whether to yourself or other people—gets in the way of happiness. Taking responsibility for your role in challenging situations, combined with a genuine quest for solutions—like reading this book, for example—is the path to empowerment and the happiness that results. In the 1982 film *Tootsie*, Teri Garr's character gives the classic line, "I'm responsible for my own orgasm!"[10] In Jack Canfield's acclaimed *The Success Principles*, the first principle is, "Take 100% Responsibility for Your Life."[11] While these are *very* different examples of taking responsibility, when you develop a solution-oriented mind-set instead of one focused on blame, you will open the door to greater satisfaction in all areas of your life.

Pay Attention to Negative Self-Talk

If you are like most people, you probably have a voice in your head that isn't always very kind. When you make a mistake, the voice might say, "There you go again," "You're so stupid," or "You never learn." If a love interest rejects you, the voice might say, "Nobody likes you," "You're a loser," or "You're so ugly." This voice in your head can give commentary all day long, and its negativity can be reinforced in your dreams at night. If this scenario sounds familiar, it's time to pay attention and correct the voice as if it were a child. You probably don't let other people speak to you that way, so why do you speak that way to yourself?

You can stop negative self-talk in its tracks by replacing it with kind and encouraging self-talk. It often helps to think of someone you love dearly, like a partner, child, or pet, and imagine how you speak to them. Here are a few alternatives:

Instead of This	Try This
"There you go again."	"Only people who don't try never fail."
"You're so stupid."	"Everyone makes mistakes."
"You never learn."	"I won't stop trying."
"You're a loser."	"I'm not for everyone."
"Nobody likes you."	"I don't want or need *everyone* to like me."
"You're so ugly."	"I have a lot of beautiful features."

Your words should be kind and encouraging. That doesn't mean you should lie to yourself. If your internal voice says you are ugly and you pop back, "I'm as pretty as Beyoncé!"—well, that's fantastic if you believe it, but it will fall flat if you don't. If you are more of a plain Jane than an Angelina Jolie or more of an average Joe than a Brad Pitt, be honest with how you feel about yourself in the moment. Replace your negative self-talk with kind, encouraging words *that you believe*. This is one of the fastest ways to see a considerable shift to more positive emotions like happiness and confidence.

Take Care of Your Physical and Energetic Body

It's hard to be happy if you are suffering from aches, pains, stiffness, and weakness. Every emotion you experience is processed through your physical and energetic (nonphysical) body. Your physical body needs no explanation. However, your energetic body probably requires some explanation. You can think of your energetic body the way you think of heat rising off the pavement on a hot day. You may not realize it, but in addition to heat, your body emits an electromagnetic field. Neuroscientist and researcher Dr. Joe Dispenza says this electromagnetic field is created based on the thoughts and feelings you have at any given moment.[12] This energy field, often referred to as an "aura," may draw people to you or repel them.

It's important to nurture your both your physical and energetic body to maintain a state of optimal happiness and wellness. All the exercises you have practiced so far—including breathwork and meditation, visualization, and journaling—are excellent support for your energetic body. Here are some other things you can do for a healthier physical body:

- **Move regularly.** You have probably heard this so many times that it's cliché. Go for a walk, take a yoga class, go for a bike ride, stand up a stretch, play tennis, play fetch with your dog, play catch with the kids, tend to a garden, try a YouTube exercise video, take a dance class, go roller-skating, go ice-skating, visit your local gym. You've got the idea. Get moving at least three times per week!
- **Eat well.** You cannot look at your smartphone, turn on the computer, watch TV, or listen to radio and podcasts without hearing advertising for weight loss programs or news reports about what you should and shouldn't eat. According to the nonprofit organization Physicians Committee for Responsible Medicine, a low-fat, whole food, plant-based diet is ideal for optimal health. Focusing your diet on fruits, vegetables, and whole grains can reduce heart

disease and cholesterol, lower cancer risk, and improve weight management.[13]

AN IMPORTANT NOTE ABOUT FORGIVENESS

You may have read books and articles or listened to radio programs, TV shows, and podcasts about the importance of forgiveness. This can be confusing, because there are two primary definitions of forgiveness: One is to offer absolution from wrongdoing and the other is to stop holding on to resentment. Now you know resentment is one of the 7 Cranky Cousins, so according to that definition, you must absolutely forgive others (release resentment) and forgive yourself (release guilt.)

When you consider forgiveness as absolving someone else from wrongdoing, that can be tricky. For clarity, unless you are a judge in a court of law or some higher power or God, you don't have the authority to absolve someone else's wrongdoing. That's not your job. You don't hold any authority over the person. Whatever your spiritual belief system is, universal law says that actions have consequences. This concept is often referred to as Karma. You don't have to accept any form of emotional or physical abuse to be a forgiving person. To forgive means to release your resentments and move on with living your best life.

CAN YOU BUILD EMPATHY?

You can certainly build empathy. Here are a few ways you can grow healthy empathy to improve your relationships and level up your joy.

Develop Self-Awareness

It may sound strange, but get to know yourself. Your sense of identity is based on a complex mix of where you were born, who raised you, what you witnessed and experienced as a child, what values were instilled in you, the education you received, the movies and television you watched, the magazines you read, and so on. Be willing to question what you think you know, even about yourself. If you could live anywhere in the world, where would it be? If you could only take one person with you, who would that be? If the sky were the limit, what work would you do for a living? Ask yourself questions instead of believing the same old answers. Underneath the layers of what your family, your country, society, and the media have told you about yourself is the beautiful divine you just waiting to be uncovered. Just by reading this book, you are well on your way to uncovering yourself and growing as a person. My book, *12 Steps to Mind-Blowing Happiness,* offers more than sixty journaling prompts and is an additional resource to consider on your self-awareness journey.

Read Memoirs and Autobiographies of People Who Are Different from You

It's not possible to walk a mile in someone else's well-worn tennis shoes unless you listen to their story. Read or listen to books written by and about people whose lives and experiences are different from yours in terms of race, ethnicity, country of origin, gender, ability, and sexual orientation. You might try:

- *I Am Malala,* by Malala Yousafzai
- *Autobiography of Malcolm X,* by Alex Haley
- *I'm Glad My Mom Died,* by Jennette McCurdy
- *Autobiography of a Yogi,* by Paramhansa Yoganda
- *Finding Me,* by Viola Davis
- *I Know Who You Are but What Am I?,* by Ali Sands
- *I Know Why the Caged Bird Sings,* by Maya Angelou
- *The Story of My Life,* by Helen Keller
- *Thinking Outside the Chrysalis: A Black Woman's Guide to Spreading Her Wings,* by Trish Ahjel Roberts

If memoirs aren't your thing, have fun with fiction. A few novels you might try are:

- *Homegoing,* by Yaa Gyasi
- *The Alchemist,* by Paulo Coelho
- *The Kite Runner,* by Khaled Hosseini

Pay special attention to oppressed and marginalized groups to which you don't belong. Understanding stories from people of diverse backgrounds will help you to learn about the eight billion people on the planet. You will grow your empathy and your perspective and become much more fun at parties. The United States is just 4.23 percent of the global population. China, the most populous country in the world, is only 18 percent of the global population. No matter where you live, there's a whole world to learn about and explore.[14] Get curious and enjoy learning about other people and cultures.

Travel with a Mind for Learning

If you can visit other cities or countries for work or pleasure, do it with a mind toward understanding and learning. Throw out the terms "third world" and "underdeveloped"; they can seem disparaging. You live in the same world as everyone else, and even if you are not far along your personal growth journey, you probably don't want anyone to call you emotionally or physically "underdeveloped." Countries impacted by colonialism and foreign rule are often "developing" nations in part because of the short time between their independence and the present date. Other countries may be deemed "developing" because they do not have a capitalist government that prioritizes industrial development and financial reward over other aspects of culture. Even when you travel within your home country, be open to understanding the experiences of people from communities that are unlike your own. Hold off on judgment until you've slid your feet into their boots, because everyone is doing the best they can including you.

Watch Foreign Films

It used to be difficult to find and view foreign films if you didn't live in a big city with an independent theater. That has changed. You can easily watch foreign films streamed directly into your home on a variety of platforms. Enjoy films the same way you would enjoy foreign travel, with a mind for learning.

Here are a few films to look for:

- *Like Water for Chocolate* (1993)
- *Amélie* (2001)
- *Train to Busan* (2016)
- *The African Doctor* (2016)
- *Like Cotton Twines* (2017)
- *The Platform* (2019)
- *Aloe Vera* (2020)

Look for genres you enjoy, then search on Google or your favorite streaming platforms. On Netflix, if you enter the name of a country that interests you, a wide range of foreign films will pop up in many genres. Variety is the spice of life. Try adding one film a month to your movie diet to broaden your understanding and add a few new flavors to your world.

Notice and Acknowledge People from Backgrounds Different than Yours

Many people go through life feeling overlooked and unseen. Make a conscious effort to notice folks and really see them as human beings, just like you. You might see someone who doesn't have a permanent place to live. Offer help if you can, but also consider their situation with empathy and kindness. What type of childhood might they have had? Did they suffer from physical, emotional, or sexual abuse? Where are their families? What might they have endured to get in such a predicament? Do they suffer from mental illness or substance addiction? Were they abandoned by their families because they are part of the LGBTQ+ community? Remember that childhood imagination? This is a great time to use it. Of course, anyone can come upon hard times and find themselves without a permanent address, so there should be no assumption of any one situation. Incredibly talented and famous people like Tyler Perry, Halle Berry, and Kelly Clarkson have publicly shared stories of being without permanent housing.[15]

Pay attention to the cashier who rings up your groceries, the server in your favorite restaurant, the folks at the fast-food drive-thru window, the guy working at the gas station, and the barista who brews up your morning latte. If there's someone in your office who is the "only" in their group: the only woman, the only Black, Hispanic, Muslim, or

Asian person, recognize their challenge. You don't have to be weird and try to become their new best friend, but you can acknowledge that the person's journey is unique and different from your own. You aren't better than anyone else. Everyone is working with the hand they have been dealt. Everyone is at a different point in their life's journey. Everyone deserves both respect and compassion.

Learn about the Animal Liberation Movement

If you live with a dog, cat, or other animal, you are likely aware of the wide range of emotions and feelings that nonhuman animals have. Nonhuman animals experience deep emotional connections, physical pain, fear, frustration, loneliness, and terror, just like humans do. They also experience joy, pleasure, and motherly love.[16] Most Americans are outraged at the thought of eating a dog or a cat but will happily eat pigs, cows, and chickens. All nonhuman animals suffer and should be treated with respect and compassion. Because of capitalist economies and a history of colonialism and slavery, systems are in place that model previous atrocities and allow for the transportation, torture, and slaughter of billions of land animals each year. Chickens fare the worst, with nearly 74 billion chickens slaughtered globally in 2021, compared to 1.4 billion pigs and 332 million cows.[17]

It is estimated that more than 90 percent of farmed animals globally are living in factory farms, including 74 percent of all land animals and virtually all farmed fish.[18] Factory farming confines large numbers of animals within small, cruelly inadequate living spaces so companies can maximize profits in selling their bodies or milk to consumers. Routine mutilation like clipping beaks, tails, and testicles without the use of painkillers are common. Antibiotic drugs are overused to combat the dangerously unsanitary living conditions. According to the World Health Organization, approximately 80 percent of medically important antibiotics are given to factory farmed animals, contributing to antibiotic resistance in humans.[19] According the US Centers for Disease Control and Prevention, antibiotic-resistant bacteria and fungi cause 2.8 million infections and thirty-five thousand deaths each year.[20] The environmental impact includes air and water pollution, global warming, deforestation, depletion of resources like water and grain, and threats to wildlife and ocean ecosystems.

As if that were not enough, there is the impact on society. Factory farms require unskilled labor and pay low wages. Undocumented and desperate workers are often hired and forced to accept the worst working conditions. This played out in 2020, when COVID-19 outbreaks caused slaughterhouse shutdowns and millions of animals were killed and discarded.[21] Factory farms aren't a boon to any neighborhood and are frequently constructed within the most vulnerable communities.

Now you can see why so many animal activists risk their own bodies to film inside slaughterhouses and protest in the streets. The consumption of meat and dairy has much wider implications than what appears at first glance. So what can you do? Continue to get educated on the subject and have fun trying a plant-based diet. Here are a few movies to enjoy if you would like to learn more:

- *Vegucated* (2011)
- *Forks over Knives* (2011)
- *Cowspiracy* (2014)
- *What the Health* (2017)
- *The Game Changers* (2018)

They are all easily accessible on streaming platforms, so get some popcorn and enjoy!

* * *

Building empathy benefits you and everyone around you, even animals! Make sure to prioritize your own needs as you develop empathy and the result will be a happier life and a deeper connection with yourself and the complex and beautiful world around you.

KEY POINTS

1. The development of empathy is closely related to personal happiness not only because of its impact on anger but because it leads to improved relationships with friends, family, acquaintances, and communities (both local and global). This improved connection and understanding can lead to a greater sense of purpose and

fulfillment, which is considered the ultimate goal of the human experience.

2. "Empath" is a pop culture term used to describe those who have difficulty prioritizing their own needs and allow feelings of empathy for others to cause them confusion and pain.

3. Healthy Empathy is marked by five main characteristics:
   - It feels good.
   - It promotes understanding.
   - It has boundaries.
   - It promotes good relationships.
   - It helps you transform anger and is a cornerstone for overall happiness.

4. Research shows that 50 percent of your happiness comes from your genetics and 10 percent comes from circumstances like wealth, relationship status, or career choice. That means **40 percent of your happiness can be changed by your behavior,** like reading this book and creating new habits and ways of thinking. Isn't that fantastic news? You can make yourself happier! Some ways of boosting your happiness quotient are:
   - Follow a path to self-actualization like that outlined in the book *12 Steps to Mind-Blowing Happiness*.
   - Mindfully appreciate your body, life, and experiences through a gratitude practice.
   - Focus on solutions instead of blaming other people or yourself.
   - Pay attention to and correct negative self-talk.
   - Take care of your physical and energetic body.

5. Much like happiness, empathy can be developed using a variety of techniques:
   - Develop self-awareness.
   - Read the memoirs of people unlike you.
   - Travel with an eye on learning.
   - Watch foreign films.
   - Acknowledge people who are different from you in background or socioeconomic stature.
   - Learn about the animal liberation movement and consider a plant-based diet.

There are a wide variety of fun and entertaining ways to grow healthy empathy. By taking the time to develop your empathy, you will open the door for healing, harmony, and increased levels of happiness in your life.

ANGER MYTHBUSTER EXERCISE

Process

1. Grab your journal or electronic device for note-taking.
2. Practice at least one of the breathing techniques you learned in chapter 5 for one minute. Feel free to try more than one or even choose a favorite. Write how you feel after trying each technique.
3. Write down your answers to the following questions:
   - Describe the last time you got angry. Did a lack of imagination or empathy play a role?
   - What was the underlying emotion (hurt, fear, embarrassment, etc.)? What was the result?
   - Which techniques for building empathy resonated the most with you?
   - Which techniques for increasing your happiness stood out for you?

Practice

- What strategies will you commit to going forward? Choose at least one that you will practice this week and write it down in your journal.

Chapter 10

It's Still Okay to Vent

Handle difficult emotions with care.

Can you imagine a life without anger? With time and practice, it is possible to transform your anger triggers so quickly that you don't rise to anger at all. But let's be real—this world has plenty of injustice, violence, and suffering. You will experience loss, grief, and illness. You might have to navigate relationships and interactions with greedy and toxic people, even family members. Even when you use the five-step Tame and Reframe approach to process your anger, you may still find yourself overwhelmed with emotions. It's important to understand that it's still okay to vent. In this chapter you will learn how to vent safely and protect your energy, so that even in the worst scenarios you can continue to manifest the life you love.

One definition of "venting" is "forceful expression or release of pent-up thoughts or feelings."[1] As you work daily to process and reframe anger and its 7 Cranky Cousins, you will find you don't harbor pent-up emotions the way you might have in the past. The Tame and Reframe technique allows you to think about and process your negative emotions, whether they are big (like rage) or smaller (like disappointment, annoyance, frustration, jealousy, impatience, guilt, and resentment). However, there may be times when you are processing something so upsetting that you would like to release your emotions in a healthy way with the help of another person. Let's explore the difference between healthy and unhealthy venting.

CHARACTERISTICS OF HEALTHY VENTING

You have probably seen people release their pent-up frustrations in an unhealthy way. Healthy venting has a few important characteristics that distinguish it from its unhealthy counterpart:

- **Healthy venting takes place in a safe space.** You might speak to an understanding friend or with a trained counselor or therapist. You want a safe space to vent so that the information you share won't be used against you later and you can feel free of judgment.
- **The receiver agrees to listen and hold space for you.** You might say, "I really need to vent. Is that okay?" You should not vent with people who haven't agreed to safely hold the space for you to do so.
- **Healthy venting is not bullying or abusive.** You may be releasing sadness, despair, disappointment, frustration and other negative emotions. However, you are not yelling and dumping your negativity on the listener. Your listener should also feel safe.
- **Healthy venting has a beginning and an end.** You might ask a loved one or a therapist to allow you to vent and work through your emotions. Whether it takes ten minutes or an hour, it should have a start and end point. Venting for days on end is no longer venting; it is an indication that you are overwhelmed by your emotions and might benefit from professional help.
- **Healthy venting leaves you feeling better than when you started.** You should feel like you've gotten help to process your emotions. The person you are venting to might ask you clarifying questions—such as "How do you feel now?" or "What do you think is the best next step?"—to help you get unstuck and find a path forward from your anger and pain.

CHARACTERISTICS OF UNHEALTHY VENTING

While healthy venting can help you process emotional overwhelm, work through solutions, and figure out next steps, unhealthy venting may cause more problems. It can make you act inappropriately and feel regret afterward. Here are some common characteristics of unhealthy venting:

- **It doesn't happen in a safe space.** You release and share negative emotions in places like work or other public spaces.
- **You don't get permission from the person you want to vent to.** You share difficult emotions without making sure the person you are speaking to is ready and able to help you process your feelings.
- **You yell and scream.** Chances are, the person you are speaking to doesn't want to be yelled at. You may be making them feel unsafe emotionally or physically. Communication doesn't get better just because it's louder.
- **It happens repeatedly.** Venting should be reserved for times when negative emotions reach an overwhelming level. You shouldn't be venting for hours and days at a time. That's beyond venting and should be addressed with a trained professional.

HEALTHY VENTING IN ACTION

Venting is perfectly healthy when it is infrequent and done appropriately and with respect. Here are a few examples of healthy venting:

1. **You lose your job.** You go to work in the morning and are asked to go to human resources for a conversation. Next thing you know, they are asking you to pack up your belongings. You got fired. You are sad, upset, humiliated, and angry. You work through your five-step Tame and Reframe process, but you are still full of emotion and want help to process it. You call one of your close friends and tell them the news. You ask if they mind if you stop by. You really feel like you need to vent. They say it's fine, so you stop by their apartment, drink some tea, and go over all your feelings on the topic. Afterward, having come to some realizations and determined your next steps, you feel better. You feel at peace. You hang out with your friend a little while longer and play a video game. Then you go home feeling supported and on a clear path forward. You aren't happy you got fired, but you know you can do what you need to do to get another job and get on with your life.

2. **Your car is totaled.** Your car is hit by a big truck while you are driving to work. You are a bit shaken, but thankfully uninjured. Your car didn't make out so well. You've had it for quite a few years, so you don't have full coverage. You don't have money for a new car right now, and the truck driver is the one in the wrong. How are you supposed to get to work now? It's a disaster. You are trying to process your anger, frustration, and confusion. You want to scream. You leave your car at an auto shop, call work to explain what happened, and take an Uber home. When your wife gets home you tell her what happened and ask if it's okay if you vent. She says it's fine, but just give her a minute to change out of her work clothes. When she comes back, she is ready to hear what happened and help you process your negative emotions. You tell her how the truck slammed right into you, how upset you were, and how you don't have coverage for the vehicle. After your conversation, you feel a little better. It's still a shock, but you've worked through a few options to get transportation and to get the truck driver to take responsibility for the damage to your vehicle.

3. **You are a victim of domestic violence.** You have been married for two years to a partner who is often verbally abusive. You have tried to defend yourself and have recommended couples therapy, but they refuse to go. This time, your partner has gone farther than usual and punched a hole in the bedroom door before slamming you against a wall. You grab your daughter, jump in your car, and head to your mother's house. You don't know where else to turn. You call your mother on the way over to tell her that you need to vent. There's a lot going on and you need to figure out what to do. Your mother says it's fine. When you arrive at the house, she pours you a glass of wine and you tell her all about the situation with your partner: the pattern of verbal abuse for years and the way he acted out violently. Your mom listens and asks questions. By the time you finish sharing everything, you feel a little better. You know you have a big problem on your hands, but you feel like you have a path forward. While at your mother's house, you reached out to a domestic violence crisis center and a family counselor and scheduled appointments. Your mother agreed to let you stay with her until it was safe to return home. By the end of

the conversation, you feel more connected to and appreciative of your mother.

4. **A family member steals your inheritance.** You are the youngest of your four siblings. Your parents named the oldest sibling as the beneficiary on all their property and financial accounts with the belief that the oldest child would take on the role of parent if anything were to happen to them and make fair decisions for the other siblings. Your parents die suddenly in a fire. The oldest sibling says your parents left everything to her and nothing for the rest of the family. You are shocked, outraged, and devastated for yourself and your other affected siblings. You have lost both parents and now you have lost the little financial stability that your parents intended to give you. You've tried to encourage your oldest sibling to think about the rest of the family and do the right thing, but she is overcome by greed and jealousy. You remember when you were a little girl and she used to babysit you and take you to the movies with her friends, how she taught you how to ride a bike and to bake chocolate chip cookies. You cannot believe she would do this to you and your siblings. You are rocked by the loss of your parents, and this is unbearable. You schedule an appointment with your therapist. When you arrive at your appointment you let your therapist know you need to vent about the situation with your sister. You tell her how much you looked up to her, how much you loved her, how deep the loss of your parents is, how deep the pain your sister is inflicting, how you can't stand what she's doing to the family, and how you don't know what to do next. Your therapist quietly nods her head. Every now and then she asks a question. When you leave, you feel a little better. You are still disgusted with your sister, but the therapist helped you understand why your sister might act that way and steps you can take to help the rest of your family move forward. You have a list of action steps, including holding a family meeting for the impacted family members and enlisting the efforts of an attorney.

5. **A family member is killed.** You were shocked to receive a phone call from your aunt telling you that your cousin was killed in a shooting on his college campus. You can barely remember what happened next, the news was so unbelievable. Your cousin was just a young person like you. He had his whole life ahead of him.

You are upset, devastated, and angry. Why does this keep hap-
pening? Who would do something like that? He was such a good
kid. Your emotions are overwhelming and you're not sure where
to turn. You call your pastor's office and request counseling, and
your church sets you up with a counselor. When you meet with
him, you tell him what happened to your cousin. You are overwhelmed with emotion. You tell him all about your cousin, how
kind he was, how you played together growing up, how shocked,
sad and lost you feel. How angry. The counselor takes time to
listen and offer additional resources. You decide to undergo
grief counseling to help you process this loss. When you leave
the office, you are still devastated by the loss, but you can see a
path forward.

As you incorporate the five-step Tame and Reframe technique into your
life, you will find less need to vent. However, healthy venting is a tool
you can access as needed with a supportive and willing participant.

HOW TO RECEIVE HEALTHY VENTING
FROM YOUR LOVED ONES

Just like you, other people want to vent, and there may be times when
people you care about want to vent to you. They may not be familiar
with the Anger Myth or the five-step Tame and Reframe technique, so
their anger may be less controlled or processed. Here are a few tips to
help you show up as a leader in your family and community and help
other people vent:

- **Check in with yourself.** You must first make sure you are healthy
  enough emotionally to create a safe environment for the person
  who wants to vent to you. You should also check to see if you are
  willing. Do you care about the person or situation enough to offer
  support and help them process their emotions? Being available to
  someone in this way is a gift, not a requirement. This type of support and nurturing is typically reserved for close friends and family
  members. If you are in a healing profession like psychotherapy,

coaching, or spiritual leadership, you may be called to hold space for your clients.

- **Set boundaries.** What are you comfortable with? For example, you might be fine with someone venting if they don't start screaming or ranting and it doesn't take more than an hour. Decide what you will and won't tolerate, and if necessary, communicate it to the person who wants to vent.
- **Pay attention to your body language.** Once you've decided to support someone in this way, it's helpful if you use body language that nonverbally communicates your support. Of course, if they are venting over the phone, this won't apply. But if they are venting in person or on a video call, this technique can be helpful. The acronym "SOLER" can help you remember to use your body to show that you are listening:
  - S—Face the person who is speaking to you *squarely*, with your face and both shoulders turned toward them.
  - O—Maintain an *open* posture with arms relaxed and not crossed over the body.
  - L—Gently *lean* in to listen.
  - E—Make sure to maintain *eye contact*.
  - R—Be *relaxed* as you listen with empathy.[2]
- **Use active listening skills.** Active listening is a useful skill in all areas of your life: parenting, career, or relationships. If you are holding space for a friend who is overwhelmed with emotion and venting, this is an excellent time to put these skills to good use:
  1. **Be mindful.** Pay attention and be respectful. That means no interrupting, daydreaming, or planning your response. It's okay to make a note of something if necessary.
  2. **Pay attention to the venter's body language.** Sometimes what people say and what they mean can be quite different. If someone says, "I'm okay," and then hangs their head and slumps down in their chair, you can safely assume they are *not* okay. Only 7 percent of communication is believed to come from the words we use; 38 percent comes from our tone and the remaining 55 percent is completely nonverbal.
  3. **Give verbal encouragement.** Let the person know they are being listened to with small encouraging words like "I understand" or "I hear you."

4. **Ask clarifying questions and paraphrase information.** Ask questions to check your understanding without judgment. Paraphrase to make sure you are following. This will also let your friend know you are listening. For example, if a friend is venting about a job loss, you might ask, "How long were you working there?" You might paraphrase, "So they fired you after you've been there for eight years, and they gave the guy who was there for three years a promotion."

5. **Ask open-ended questions.** Because open-ended questions cannot be answered with a simple yes or no, they give the person venting an opportunity to process their feelings more completely. You might ask, "How does this make you feel?" or, "What are some steps you could take to move forward?" or even, "What can I do to support you during such a difficult time?"

6. **Refrain from judgment.** Unless the person venting to you is confessing murder, rape, or some other heinous crime, give them grace. Be open, try to remain neutral, and avoid criticizing them. Ideally, you will be able to offer them support and loving guidance.

7. **Take time for reflection.** At the end of the conversation, take some time to summarize and reflect on what was shared. Perhaps there is a clearer path forward now that the person has had some space to process difficult emotions.[3]

Learning to process your emotions and help people you care about process theirs creates intimacy in close relationships. In clinical or business relationships, it can increase respect. Take the time to use and practice these skills to improve communication in all your relationships.

WHAT ABOUT THE LAW OF ATTRACTION?

You may have heard people talk about the law of attraction, or perhaps you read *The Secret* by Rhonda Byrne[4] or saw the film of the same name. So what is all the fuss about? The idea of the law of attraction aligns perfectly with the Anger Myth. The law of attraction says that thoughts become things; consequently, negative thoughts become negative things. In Chapter 1 you learned why anger never gives desirable results. It is a negative thought, and the more time you spend dancing with negativity, the more likely the outcome will not be good.

If you consider the process of creation, you recognize that anything you might create in your life begins with a thought. You might decide to buy a house, change jobs, find a life partner, or start a business. In virtually every instance, you must first generate the desire for the thing you wish to manifest. On the contrary, if you spend your time thinking about past toxic relationships, failures, losses, and things you don't want to happen, it is far more likely that more negativity will come into your life. You must learn to control your thoughts. By reading and working through the exercises in this book, you have learned to gain control of your thoughts by redirecting and reframing your anger. Another great way to learn to control your thoughts is through meditation.

Neuroscience researcher and author Dr. Joe Dispenza says thoughts are electric and feelings are magnetic.[5] In *The Secret*, Byrne bundles this idea into one: It's your thoughts that are magnetic. No matter how you look at it, your thoughts and the resultant feelings set a blueprint for your life. In the same way that you can't be angry and happy at the same time, you also cannot constantly think negative thoughts about anger, victimization, loss, loneliness and expect your life to look any different. You must learn to control your thoughts.

In Chapter 5, you learned breathing techniques to calm your nervous system when you are presented with an anger trigger. Learning to meditate will help you create space between trigger and response and gain more control over your thoughts. Remember, negative thoughts impact your life in a real way. In the following section, you will learn some meditation techniques you can use to create more space between thought and response, make the five-step Tame and Reframe process easier, and help you think more positive thoughts and attract positive results into your life.

MEDITATIONS TO HELP YOU
CONTROL YOUR THOUGHTS

Simple Breathing Meditation

Use your smartphone or some other device as a timer. Keep a journal or electronic notepad near you. Find a space that is quiet and free from distractions. If that's not possible, tell yourself that any background noises are like white noise and that you won't follow the noises with your thoughts. Sit comfortably. Make sure your back is straight and your chin is at a 90-degree angle with your body. (No need to do math, just maintain good posture and don't slouch.) If you are comfortable closing your eyes, go ahead and close them gently. If closing your eyes makes you uncomfortable, keep them slightly open with an unfocused gaze about two feet in front of you. Place your hands, with palms facing either down or up, gently on your knees. Choose a hand posture that feels best to you. Hands down is considered a grounding posture for times of uncertainty or instability; hands up is considered an open posture for inspiration and guidance. There are many hand postures, but these are the simplest and most accessible.

Next, simply bring your awareness to your breath. Your breath will be the anchor of your meditation. This means it will be the single point of your focus. Don't try to change your breathing, just notice the sensation of air as it enters and leaves your body. Be curious. See if you can notice the sensation of air exiting and leaving your body right at the tip of your nostrils. You might notice the sensation against the hairs in your nose. You might notice that the air is cooler on your inhalation and warmer on your exhalation after it has comingled with the warmth of your body. See if you are breathing through one nostril more than the other. Be curious and notice. If you find your mind wandering, speak gently to yourself and redirect you thoughts back to your breath.

Continue to notice your breath to the exclusion to any other thought. As thoughts pop up in your mind simply say, "I see you," but don't follow the thought. Be kind to yourself by saying, "That's okay. I am learning" as you redirect your thoughts back to your breath.

Continue this pattern for between three and twenty minutes. When your meditation is complete, take out your journal or electronic device and write down a few notes about your experience.

Transcendental (Mantra) Meditation

Begin in the same way as a simple breathing meditation. Use something to track your time. You might use the stopwatch on your smartphone. Have a notepad nearby for when you complete your meditation. Find a space that is mostly free from distraction, and if that's not possible, make the commitment to ignore background noises. Sit comfortably with good posture. Close your eyes if you are comfortable doing so. Choose a hand posture, palms up or down. You may also consider a hand posture, or mudra, called the "chin mudra." In this posture, the palms are up, with the index finger and thumb gently touching. This posture symbolizes your desire to connect your spiritual self with God or the Universe. Give it a try, see how you feel, and do what feels best in your body.

Choose a mantra for your meditation. The Sanskrit "So hum" is a popular choice. Loosely translated it means "I am." If you prefer, you can simply say, "I am," as your mantra. Your mantra will serve as the anchor of your meditation. It will be the single point of your focus. Begin your meditation by bringing your awareness to your breath. When you find a rhythm, silently introduce your mantra. You might inhale "I" or "So" and exhale "Am" or "Hum." Try this out for a few breaths. If you find your mind wandering, bring it back to your chosen mantra. Continue to inhale and exhale your mantra, redirecting your mind as necessary with love and compassion, as if you were talking to a loved one (because you *are* a loved one). Don't worry if your mind wanders. It takes some practice to stay on track.

If unexpected thoughts pop up, simply acknowledge them briefly and redirect your thoughts back to your chosen mantra. Continue this pattern for between three and twenty minutes. When you feel as though your meditation is complete, make a note of your experience in your journal or electronic device.

Simple Guided Imagery Meditation

Begin in the same way as you did in the previous mediations. Use the stopwatch on your smartphone or some other mechanism to track your time. Keep a notepad handy to record your experience. Find a space that is conducive to meditation. Sit comfortably with good posture. Close your eyes if that feels good to you. Choose a hand posture, palms up or down. You may also try a traditional Kadampa Buddhist hand posture: Rest the right palm up in the left palm, which is also facing up. Gently touch the thumbs together. This signifies the hand of compassion resting in the hand of wisdom. Give it a try and see if you enjoy the hand positioning. Any hand position you are comfortable with is fine, and now you have four options.

Bring your awareness to your breath and breathe normally. Your breath will be the anchor of your meditation. This means it will be the single point of your focus. Don't try to change your breathing, just notice the sensation of air as it enters and leaves your body. If you find your mind wandering, speak gently to yourself and redirect yourself back to your breath. Continue to notice your breath. After a few rounds of breathing, imagine you are exhaling thick, dark smoke and with it any negative emotions, anger, worry, fear, mental busyness, and any physical ailments. Continue this pattern, inhaling normally and exhaling negative emotions as thick, dark smoke.

After a few rounds, imagine on your next inhalation that you are inhaling golden radiant light through the crown of your head and with every inhalation you bring in positive emotions, inspiration, abundance, focus, clarity, physical and mental wellness. Imagine inhaling joy, peacefulness, and love.

Continue with this cycle, exhaling any emotions that are troubling and inhaling calm, productive, and enlightening emotions. Take time to notice the sense of peace that arises. Then imagine that you are so consumed by this light of good, positive emotions that you begin to emanate them, so that anyone who comes near you feels this positive energy. Continue to practice this visualization. You may notice that your negative emotions have dissipated significantly. Enjoy this feeling of peace.

Continue this pattern for between three and twenty minutes. When your meditation is complete, take out your journal or electronic device and write down a few notes about your experience.

MORE BENEFITS OF MEDITATION

Meditation trains your mind to do one thing at a time and to focus on the positive. It helps you develop control of your thoughts while creating space between your thoughts and responses. It is very helpful in giving you control over your responses to anger triggers in your day-to-day life.

Besides helping you to manage anger and be happier and more peaceful, meditation offers vast mental and physical health benefits. Studies show that meditation reduces stress, anxiety, and depression. It slows the aging of the brain, supports the immune system, improves sleep, reduces pain, normalizes blood pressure, and lowers the risk of heart disease.[6]

MORE WAYS TO MANAGE YOUR THOUGHTS

The things you think about have a lot to do with your environment and what you are exposed to. What are you allowing into your mind? Are you consuming a lot of violence, pornography, stupidity, or negativity? Here are a few ways to generate more positive thoughts:

- Listen to positive, productive, and encouraging podcasts and radio shows. You might enjoy *Dear Gabby*, *Hello Seven*, or my own *Mind-Blowing Happiness Podcast*.
- Watch interesting, informative, and compassionate films and movies. Learn from documentaries like *Happy* and *The Game Changers*.[7]
- Listen to positive and uplifting music. You can find my *12 Steps to Mind-Blowing Happiness* playlist on Spotify.
- Read positive and informative books. Don't stop with *The Anger Myth*.
- Use journalistic news sources for your news content: NPR, PBS, the *Wall Street Journal*, the *New York Times*, Democracy Now, Al Jazeera, ABC, CBS, NBC, BBC, and so on.
- Consider creating a visual representation of what you want in your life with an electronic vision board that can be the wallpaper on your phone or laptop. Canva (www.canva.com) offers free templates.

HANDLE YOUR EMOTIONS WITH CARE

Emotions can run the gamut from mild and delightful to intense, painful, and everything in between. Learning to manage your thoughts and emotions is an important part of your overall health and well-being. Understanding how to vent in a healthy way, offer support when loved ones need it, and manage your thoughts using meditation and other methods will help you create the peaceful, happy, and productive life you desire. You are creating the mental habits that produce a sustainable and joyful life.

KEY POINTS

1. Venting is helpful when you learn how to do it in a healthy way. Healthy venting feels safe for both you and the person you are venting to, it's not abusive in any way, it takes place within specific time parameters, and it leaves you feeling better than when you started.
2. The law of attraction says that thoughts become things. Therefore, stewing in negative thoughts creates negative outcomes in your life. It's to your benefit to learn to control your thoughts so that you can spend more time in positivity and manifest the things that you want.
3. Learning to meditate can help you get control of your thoughts. Negative thoughts have a real impact on your life, and it's not a good one. Learning to meditate will help you attract positive results into your life. Meditation also offers a long list of physical and mental health benefits like stress reduction, improved immune system, and lower risk of heart disease.
4. Your thoughts are impacted by what you allow into your environment. Listen to positive music and media and consider creating an electronic vision board to keep positive images in front of you on a consistent basis.

We live in a complex world with beautiful art, masterful music, ingenious technology, and stunning architecture alongside weapons of mass destruction, torture devices, inhumane prisons, and cruel factory farms.

At some point in your life, you will experience loss and grief. There will likely be times when you will want to express intense emotions in a safe way. Repressing your emotions is never helpful. It's important to learn to vent in a healthy way, so that even on your most difficult days you can continue to process your emotions and manifest the joyful life you desire.

ANGER MYTHBUSTER EXERCISE

Process

1. Grab your journal or electronic device for note-taking.
2. Practice each of the three meditation exercises you learned in this chapter for a minimum of three minutes. Write how you feel after trying each technique.
- Write down your answers to the following questions:
  - When was the last time you vented? What was the outcome? Do you think it was healthy or unhealthy venting?
  - Which example of healthy venting resonated with you most? Who is the person or people with whom you can safely vent to if necessary? What people can vent safely with you?
  - Which meditation technique(s) do you like the most?
  - How do you think the music and media you consume impacts you?

Practice

- Over the next few days, try incorporating a minimum of three minutes of daily meditation into your routine.
- Notice if and how you need to vent. Is it healthy?
- Take inventory of the music and media in your life. Incorporate more positive entertainment and accurate news reporting where possible.

Chapter 11

The Blissful Side Effects

Now that you are in control, who will you choose to be?

Can you imagine a life free from anger? When you started reading this book, you probably couldn't picture it. Now you have all the resources necessary to remove anger from your life completely. You've learned the five-step Tame and Reframe technique, simple breathwork and meditation methods, how to employ your empathy, healthy venting guidelines, and alot of strategies to keep your mind positive. Now it's time to enjoy the blissful side effects of the work you have done and will continue to do. This chapter will give you the opportunity to explore what your life can look like now that you are in more control of your negative emotions. You have opened the door to new possibilities. Make no mistake about it: understanding the Anger Myth is powerful, and you will experience a positive shift in your life and your worldview.

When you were a child, chances are you were asked at least once what you wanted to be when you grew up. If you were like most children, you might have chosen something aspirational, like an astronaut, president, ballerina, or football player. As you grew into an adult, you probably let go of your childhood dreams and sought more practical endeavors. You might have gone from believing anything is possible as a child to having very limited beliefs about what is possible as an adult. In life coaching, limiting beliefs are negative things you believe to be true that on further examination are not true at all. A limiting belief you may have had before reading this book is that anger is necessary and useful. On further examination, you have learned that anger isn't necessary or helpful at all. The faster you can transform it into either peace or constructive action, the more productive and enjoyable your life will be.

LIMITING VERSUS EMPOWERING BELIEFS

Limiting beliefs hold us back, while empowering beliefs drive us forward. But how do you know if you have limiting beliefs standing between you and the life of your dreams? How are they formed? How do you get rid of them? If you have goals that you've always wanted to achieve and haven't, chances are there are limiting beliefs at the root.

Limiting beliefs can be formed in a variety of ways:

- **Childhood:** Your parents are your first teachers. They may have taught you some of your limiting beliefs. Perhaps they said you aren't smart or pretty. Maybe they set an expectation for your career options. Perhaps they communicated by yelling and screaming. As a child, it is natural to believe what your parents tell you and model for you, but parents have limiting beliefs too. It's important to question those early lessons.
- **Social Circle:** The people you know through family, friends, and community taught you what is possible for you, probably without you even realizing it. You are most likely to believe what you have seen with your own eyes. So if you want to be a world-class chef, but you've only met the guy who flips burgers at your local diner, it's difficult to imagine becoming a successful chef. That could be true for being a doctor, lawyer, musician, or any other role that you consider a dream job.
- **Life Events:** Major life experiences impact our belief systems and may create limiting beliefs. For example, if you have a wonderful marriage, you might believe people who have been single for a long time are unstable. If you received a big promotion, you might believe people who struggle financially don't work as hard as you do. If you experienced a negative life event, like a robbery in a mall or a business failure, you may believe malls or business start-ups are inherently unsafe.

Limiting beliefs form as a way of protecting us from harm, and over time they can narrow our capacity for growth until we find ourselves feeling stuck or unhappy. If you have goals that you haven't achieved and maybe aren't even working toward, you can be confident that limiting beliefs are in play. You already pushed past a common limiting belief about anger by reading this book and working through the exercises. Here's how you can get rid of more of these pesky dream-killers and replace them with empowering beliefs:

- **Give yourself permission to dream.** In Chapter 6, you learned to gear up your imagination; now use that imagination to dream. You might be scared to dream because you are afraid of failure. It may sound harsh, but living a life without dreams is already a failure, so you have nothing to lose. Pull out your journal and write down what you really want to see in your life. Where do you want to live? What kind of work do you want to do? What kind of friends and relationships do you want to have? Who do you want to impact? In his book *Awaken the Giant Within*, world-renowned motivational speaker Tony Robbins says, "The quality of your life is a direct reflection of the quality of the questions you are asking yourself."[1] So ask yourself some questions and don't be afraid of your answers.
- **Become a lifelong learner.** We live in a time with incredible access to data. Read books that inspire and encourage you, like referenced in earlier chapters and listed in the resources section at the end of this book. Read the positive and inspirational stories of people who don't look or sound like you. Follow the blogs and podcasts of positive thought leaders who set an example and provide resources to help you reach your goals.
- **Replace limiting words with empowering ones.** That little voice in your head is often noisy and busy, but remember: you are the boss. Replace "I can't" with "I won't" or "I will" and reclaim your power. Your self-talk should always be two things: kind and empowering. So if you hear the voice in your head say something mean, quickly correct it with kindness and compassion, as if you were teaching a child or someone that you love.
- **Visualize the future you want.** You learned to visualize in Chapter 5. Take time on a regular basis to practice visualization. In Chapter 9, you learned that your thoughts and feelings create an electromagnetic field or "aura" around you that you share with the surrounding biosphere. No matter what you call it, when you visualize your desired future, you elevate your energy field and increase the likelihood that your desires will manifest.

- **Don't be afraid to ask for help.** It seems counterintuitive, but asking for help can be the ultimate in courage. Reach out to supportive friends and mentors and build a community of like-minded people who want to find passion and purpose in life. Consider working with a life coach, counselor, or therapist. Support is critical for success.

Limiting beliefs can make you miss out on the life you really want. Summon up the courage to dream, be a lifelong learner, embrace empowering words, visualize your best future ever, and get in a community of like-minded folks to attain your most meaningful, power-packed, and juiciest life. You deserve it.

FINDING YOUR PASSION

What are you most passionate about? Can you bring more passion and purpose into your life? When you live a meaningful, passion-driven life, you can get past obstacles more easily. You will be so focused on your calling that small things won't bother you the way they might have in the past. The five-step Tame and Reframe method taught you how to respond to your anger triggers. Finding passion and purpose in your life will help you to have fewer triggers to begin with.

You probably grew up watching cartoons and movies featuring princesses and superheroes. While princesses weren't typically very powerful, superheroes often had special powers, whether it was super strength, the ability to fly, see through walls, or climb the side of buildings. Much like superheroes, every person has their own superpowers. They might not be as dramatic as seeing through walls or flying, but they can be just as powerful. Developing the ability to identify your superpowers is a big step toward creating the life that you most desire.

Your superpowers are the activities you enjoy doing and are very talented at. It might be cooking, writing, speaking, caring for children, gardening, singing, drawing, or other endeavors. In Chapter 8, you read profiles of successful businesspeople who were able to convert an annoyance into multimillion-dollar businesses. They not only identified their superpowers, they also honed in on the audience they wanted to serve. Madam C. J. Walker served Black women. Steve Jobs began by serving college students and later took the world by storm. Sara Blakely served women. Pinky Cole served urban communities. Rachel Rodgers served marginalized and underrepresented entrepreneurs. They were all driven by passion and purpose.

In *Change Your Habits, Change Your Life*, author Tom Corley states that pursuing your own long-term dreams and goals can result in both happiness and the creation of wealth—as was the case with all the entrepreneurs profiled in Chapter 7.[2] This is yet another reason why it's important to understand your passions and create meaning in your life beyond mere survival. (In case you are wondering, having children and building a family is part of survival.) In Buddhist philosophy it is understood that even the smallest of animals have the desire to be happy and free from suffering—to survive and avoid pain. If you observe even small insects, you will notice this is true. You have probably seen ants working together or birds flying in unison. You've seen insects run for their lives while you or someone else was attempting to kill them. **Survival is the smallest of goals. Humans have the capacity to access their spirituality and intellect to pursue profoundly meaningful goals. Don't sell yourself short.**

Think back to your childhood. What did you most enjoy doing? Were you good at sports? Did you talk a lot? Swimming with the current of what naturally brings you joy will produce more fulfillment and purpose in your life. Do you imagine life as an entrepreneur, or do you prefer to have someone else make the big decisions?

You were introduced to psychologist Abraham Maslow's theory of psychological health based on the hierarchy of needs in Chapter 9. The pinnacle of Maslow's hierarchy is self-actualization, or the fulfillment of your highest potential—in other words, finding your passion and purpose. Only you can decide what that is. Authors Jim Collins and Jerry Porras coined the term "Big Hairy Audacious Goal"—or BHAG—in their book *Built to Last: Successful Habits of Visionary Companies.*[3] While their term was initially developed for companies, anyone can create their own BHAG (pronounced "bee-hag"). Creating your own personal BHAG can serve as your focus point, North Star, or life's purpose. You may never reach your BHAG, but you will be clear about what direction to go. You may have heard the old Norman Vincent Peale quote, "Shoot for the moon, even if you miss, you'll land among the stars."[4] Your BHAG can get you excited and point you in the right direction for years. If you are lucky enough to achieve your BHAG, you simply create a new one. Here are some famous BHAGS you might recognize:

- Microsoft's mission was to "put a computer on every desk in every home."
- NASA's BHAG was to "put a man on the Moon." Now NASA's new goal is to colonize Mars.
- Amazon's mission was to "make any book, in any language, available in less than a minute."
- Netflix had the bold vision to become the first video-streaming service in the world.
- Walmart's BHAG was to "become a $125 billion company by the year 2000."[5]

For individuals, BHAGs like this simply may not apply. So what could a BHAG look like for you? Here are a few ideas:

- Play your favorite sport or instrument in a big arena or stage in the next ten years.
- Create a foundation for your favorite charity in fifteen years.
- Have a million dollars in your bank account in eight years.
- Help one hundred kids attend college by the time you retire.
- Become a CEO for a major corporation in ten years.
- Teach the 12 Steps to Mind-Blowing Happiness to twelve million people in twelve years. (You guessed it—that one is mine!)

Now that you have the idea, take some time to think about what you want most in life besides survival. If you could do more anything you wanted, what would you do?

KEY POINTS

1. Limiting beliefs hold us back, while empowering beliefs drive us forward. If you have unrealized goals, chances are there are limiting beliefs at the root. Limiting beliefs can be formed in a variety

of ways. They are typically formed as a defense mechanism from three main sources: childhood, your social circle, or life events.
2. You can replace limiting beliefs with empowering ones by taking action:
   • Give yourself permission to dream.
   • Become a lifelong learner.
   • Replace limiting words with empowering ones.
   • Visualize the future you want.
   • Don't be afraid to ask for help.
3. Much like superheroes, every person has their own superpowers. Your superpowers are the activities you enjoy doing and are very talented at. Developing the ability to identify your superpowers is a big step toward creating the life that you most desire.
4. Finding your passion and purpose is your birthright. The smallest insects look out for their families, avoid pain, and work to survive. Survival is the tiniest of goals. Humans are spiritual and intellectual beings with the capacity to pursue profoundly meaningful goals.
5. Creating your own Big Hairy Audacious Goal can help you find your purpose. It can serve as your focus point or North Star. Even if you don't reach your BHAG, it will give you clarity on which direction to go.

Using the tools you have learned to manage negative thoughts and emotions, you can create space for passion, purpose, and the realization of your fullest potential. Whether you choose to be an entrepreneur, a cook, a gardener, or any combination of identities, you have freed up the room in your heart and mind to dream the life you want to live. Enjoy the blissful side effects of an anger-free life.

ANGER MYTHBUSTER EXERCISE

Process:

1. Grab your journal or electronic device for note-taking.
2. Practice your favorite breathwork or meditation for three minutes. Write how you feel. Allow yourself some extra time to work on this section, and come back to it as many times as you would like.

3. Write a list of limiting beliefs you have about yourself, and then go back and challenge yourself to see if they are true. Make note of any epiphanies. Your list might look something like this:

   • I'm not very smart. (Challenge: I graduated high school, so I'm probably average; or I've been working full time for ten years, so I'm smart enough to hold down a job. Maybe I am pretty smart.)

   • I don't come from money. (Challenge: I live in one of the richest countries in the world and I have access to the internet and public libraries, so I'm not that poor; or I come from a middle-class family, which in many parts of the world would be considered rich. Wait—maybe I *do* come from money.)

4. Write a list of things you love to do. If you can't think of anything, go back to the things you loved as a child. Then circle the things you know you are talented at. (If you're not sure, ask your friends and family.) This is the list of your superpowers. Feel free to add to your list later. Make a note of which of your superpowers could be most lucrative.

5. Write down the communities or populations you most want to serve. It could be women, farmers, social justice activists, young men, or any other group that's near and dear to your heart. It may be a community with which you identify.

6. Now look at the list of superpowers and the list of communities you want to serve. Does anything jump out at you? How can you blend your unique list of superpowers with your passion to serve a group of people? Have fun creating multiple purpose statements or BHAGs.

7. Write your obituary or "future self essay." What would you like to be remembered for? Write it down.

Practice

• After you have finished working on your exercises to identify your passion and life's purpose, notice how you feel as you move through your day with this new knowledge.

Chapter 12

Welcome to the Good Life

Your most peaceful home resides within your mind.

Do you want the best life possible for you and your family? You have probably heard stories of wealthy people who kill themselves and poor people who relish and enjoy their lives. It may seem counterintuitive, but happiness and peace aren't dependent upon what you possess in life—they reside within your own mind. This is not to say that you shouldn't work to achieve wealth or anything your heart desires. Afterall, now you have a Big Hairy Audacious Goal and the passion and purpose to move you forward. Even if you are not 100 percent there, you certainly have a workable blueprint. But no matter what you do or don't have, you can find solace within yourself. You can make a commitment in each moment to enjoy your life, pursue your dreams, lean into faith and compassion, and show up each day with the hope of great things to come. But what does an amazing life really look like? You can learn the parameters of a good life and decide to make any necessary adjustments to create your own best life.

In life coaching, there are a variety of templates to assess the quality of your life. The Eight Main Life Areas is one such framework.

THE EIGHT MAIN LIFE AREAS

1. **Mental Health and Personal Development:** This life area covers your level of self-awareness and mental wellness as well as your level of interest in improving yourself personally. In Chapter 4, you learned that self-awareness can range from how

you see yourself to your understanding of how others see you. Commitment to your personal growth and mental health is one of the most important aspects of a healthy and balanced life.

2. **Relationships:** This life area includes all your relationships with people, whether they are partners and love interests, family, friends, coworkers, or acquaintances. Robust, varied, and meaningful relationships are necessary for survival and paramount for a thriving, fulfilling, and joyful life.

3. **Physical Health:** This life area covers the health of your physical body as distinguished from your mental health. It includes the current state of your physical body as well as the activities you rely on to maintain physical wellness. This might include regular visits to the doctor, a workout routine, proper nutrition, and more.

4. **Spiritual Life:** This life area is important whether you consider yourself religious or not. You can be religious and not spiritual, spiritual and not religious, or both spiritual and religious. This life area includes any awareness, support, and nourishment of your nonphysical, energetic, or spiritual self and its connection to the universe, a higher power, or God. This area might include religious affiliations and activities like attending a church, mosque, or temple. It also can also include reading spiritual texts and participating in activities to explore your divine consciousness, like yoga, prayer, meditation, spiritual retreats, spiritual groups, sweat lodges, and more. Always be careful when exploring your spirituality. Unfortunately, there are so-called spiritual leaders who take advantage of vulnerable people looking for spiritual support. Make sure to use critical thinking skills and do your research. There is a whole section on how to do just that in the appendix at the end of this book.

5. **Occupation:** This life area is usually your paid employment, but it can also be unpaid work like maintaining a household or significant volunteer work. Your occupation is how you spend most of your time, whether working a full-time job, balancing a part-time job with family, full-time volunteer responsibilities, or anything in between.

6. **Fun and Recreation:** This is an important life area that for many people goes unnoticed. The exploration of and participation in enjoyable hobbies and activities is a large component of what

makes life most satisfying. Happy people with working imaginations are never bored. Fun and recreation could be sports, art, spending time with friends and family, going to movies or shows, taking walks in nature, or just about any fun thing your mind can come up with. It can also be watching TV or movies at home, reading books, playing video games, or gardening. The list is endless. Make sure you have a healthy list of fun activities that you enjoy.

7. **Money:** Financial circumstances is one of the areas that people worry about most. However, this life area isn't only about financial stability, it is also about perspective. Each person's idea of financial stability or financial freedom is different. And perspective plays a huge role. For example, an artist on the rise with very little money in their bank account may feel very comfortable, while a retired executive who lost most of his retirement assets due to a market downturn may feel very uncomfortable.

8. **Physical Environment:** This life area has changed quite a bit since the 2020 pandemic, when remote work became much more common. Your physical environment consists of your home space and your neighborhood, and it also includes your workspace and your work neighborhood if you work outside the home. This area doesn't involve any people you might live or work with. (They are part of the relationships life area.)

THE EIGHT MAIN LIFE AREAS
AND PURPOSE IN ACTION

When the Eight Main Life Areas are in balance and combined with a sense of purpose, you will have a new level of joy and fulfillment in your life. Now that you are in control of your negative emotions, you have identified your superpowers, and you know (or are close to knowing) your North Star, you can experience pure magic in your life. Let's look at a few examples of how this might look.

- Mindy S. loved her work as a nurse, but she felt something was missing in her life. After working through the Eight Main Life Areas with her life coach, she realized she had a lot of job satisfaction, but she didn't take time to take care of her mental or spiritual health. She was in a healthy ten-year relationship, had a great group of friends, and loved her home, but she had unresolved trauma that gave her bouts of anxiety and depression. Sometimes her solution was to use work as a distraction, which resulted in overworking. Working with her coach helped build a healthier, more balanced life. She became more self-aware, hired a therapist, and began exploring spiritual books and practices. With the help of her coach, she realized that she most enjoyed working with the elderly and transitioned from being an ER nurse to working in a nursing home. She realized that one of her superpowers was her beautiful voice, so she developed a program in her hospital to bring live music to the patients on her floor once a week. She received amazing feedback from the patients and families she served. It brought her to tears of joy. She couldn't be happier.

- Timothy K. worked in advertising sales, but he struggled with anger and heavy drinking. A counselor at his church introduced him to the Eight Main Life Areas. When he reflected on them, he realized he was religious, but he wasn't spiritual. He attended church and took communion on Sundays with his family, but he didn't think of himself as a nonphysical, spiritual being in communication with the nonphysical world. His counselor encouraged him to learn to meditate to create more of a connection with his spiritual self. He also realized that his anger was rooted in a sense of obligation to his family that made him work a job he didn't enjoy. He spoke to his wife and his friends to help him identify his superpowers. He realized he was quite good at sales and persuasion, and he could probably sell anything. He also really enjoyed gadgets and technology. He hired a career coach to help him chart a path from advertising sales to tech sales. His anger subsided and he didn't want to drink as much. He began spending the weekends in nature with his family, which they all enjoyed. He was able to be more loving with them once he let go of the sense of obligation and resentment he had been carrying for years.

- Shaina W. worked as a human resources director for a large multinational corporation. She was single, worked long hours, and made well above six figures. But she was about to turn forty and longed for a husband and children, and she didn't see any hope for her to have the family she had always dreamed of. All her previous relationships had ended badly. She was participating in a career-coaching program with her employer when she was introduced to the Eight Main Life Areas. She realized that while her money and occupation were very good, her relationships and fun were not good at all. The career coach referred her to a transformational coach for help. The new coach helped her identify what she really enjoyed doing and had her make a commitment to do more of those things. She started roller-skating and riding her bicycle. Not long after, she joined skating and cycling groups. One of the friends in her new skating group introduced her to the man who would become her husband. She loved the work she did in human resources advocating for employees and candidates and didn't want to leave, but she wanted to work fewer hours and start a family. She worked with her career coach to help her redesign her career so she could work less while she focused on starting a family. By the time she turned forty-three, she had the husband and child she had always wanted. Instead of waiting for life to happen to her, she learned to advocate for her own dreams.

- Bennett C. had been working in a warehouse for the past five years. It was his first job out of high school, and he stayed with the company while his friends went off to college, leaving him behind. He found a book in the library that introduced him to the Eight Main Life Areas and the idea of having a purpose or North Star. He knew that money was a big problem for him, but he hadn't thought seriously about charting a path to a new occupation. He never liked school and English was his second language, so part of him had given up. He realized he needed to invest more time into his mental health and personal development, and he needed to work on his occupation and money situation. He used to love woodworking classes in school. He liked to work with his hands, so he googled job opportunities for carpenters and plumbers. He researched what was required, spoke to family members, and contacted companies. After some time, his father's friend reached out to him saying he had weekend work on a construction site. This got Bennett's foot in the door. He started working part-time and eventually landed a union job with great pay, which allowed him to quit his warehouse position. He loved building things and he wanted to give back to his community, so he volunteered to build furniture for a local homeless shelter. He was doing work he loved, getting paid well, and contributing to his community. He felt like he had found his purpose, and he no longer compared himself to what his classmates were doing. He was amazed how much that one book changed his life, and he committed himself to reading more books and listening to more podcasts for his personal development. He loved his life and looked forward to one day having a family and maybe even starting his own business.

There is no limit to the ways that the knowledge of the Eight Main Life Areas can impact you when combined with passion and purpose. Now you have all the tools to create the life you have always dreamed of, whether you want to have a family, change careers, or travel the world. When your Eight Main Life Areas are harmonious and purposeful, your life will be juicier.

* * *

You did the work! You read the chapters and did the exercises. You practiced what you learned. Now *you* are in control of your negative emotions. They don't control you. You've learned your superpowers. You are focused on your North Star. You have created space in your life for truly living—for more than just surviving, but living with joy.

Now that you understand the Anger Myth, you are free to craft the life you've always wanted.

KEY POINTS

1. The Eight Main Life Areas—mental health and personal development, relationships, physical health, spiritual life, occupation, fun and recreation, money, and your physical environment—are a helpful framework to assess your life.
2. When the Eight Main Life Areas are balanced and combined with a sense of purpose, you will experience pure magic in your life. A balanced life with a sense of purpose and direction is a game changer.

ANGER MYTHBUSTER EXERCISE

Process

1. Grab your journal or electronic device for note-taking.
2. Practice your favorite breathwork or meditation for three minutes. Write how you feel.
3. Rate each of your Eight Main Life Areas on a scale from one to ten, with one being the lowest and ten the highest. A score of one may indicate you don't have awareness of that area in your life at all—like, "What's healing?"—whereas a score of ten shows mastery—like, "I am aware of my past trauma, and I've done the work to heal. I feel whole and complete."
4. Take note of your three lowest scores and write your answers to these questions for each of those life areas.
   - What can I set as a goal for this area of my life for three months from now? (Make sure your goals are specific, measurable, attainable, and emotionally relevant to you.)
   - What action steps can I take this week to move me toward my goal?

Your list might look like this:

Mental and Personal Development	4
	My goal for three months from now is to feel happier and more healed from past trauma. I won't be controlled by anger and negative emotions. I'll be able to measure it because I will experience a whole month without complaining or fussing. I can also rate the Eight Main Life Areas again to see where I am.
	This week I can research my options and schedule an appointment with a therapist.
Relationships	7
Physical Health	9

Spiritual Life	4
	My goal for three months from now is to feel a connection to my spiritual self and have some sort of daily spiritual practices in place that nourish and support me. In three months, it should be consistent for at least five days a week for the previous two months. I can also rate this area again at the end of the three months to track my progress.
	My action step for this week is to research spiritual books and find one to listen to on audiobook.
Occupation	8
Fun and Recreation	5
	My goal for three months from now is to have hobbies and fun activities that I engage in on a regular basis. I'll know I reached my goal when I have done two fun activities per month for three months.
	My action step for this week is to research some of the activities I enjoyed as a child: drawing, painting, and riding my bike. I will identify opportunities in my neighborhood.
Money	8
Physical Environment	8

Practice

Once you have identified one, two, or three of the Eight Main Life Areas that you want to work on, practice your action steps for the week. If you are committed to making positive changes in your life, enlist the support of a life coach or a friend to work with as an accountability partner. If you don't have access to someone like that in your life, schedule a day each week for self-coaching. On that day you can review your results for the previous week and set new action steps for the upcoming week. Every three months, set new goals. You are intentionally learning and growing. Say goodbye to anger.

Now you have all the tools to understand and overcome the mental habits that steal your joy. You have successfully processed and practiced all the lessons of the Anger Myth. Welcome to the good life

Appendix

Finding Info in the Age of Disinformation

"Believe nothing, no matter where you read it or who said it, no matter if I have said it, unless it agrees with your own reason and your own common sense."

—Buddha

In this book, you learned to transform your anger into constructive action by using the Three E's: Entertainment, Education, and Enlightenment. But how do you do proper research when there is so much misinformation and disinformation out there?

It's important to understand the distinction between these two very important terms:

Misinformation is incorrect information, typically given by accident.

Disinformation is false information spread on purpose to deceive people.

One of the greatest recent examples disinformation in the United States is the dissemination of what is now referred to as the Big Lie: the narrative that the 2020 US presidential election was stolen. As of this writing, thousands of people believe the Big Lie because they do not know how to identify credible news sources or use critical thinking skills.

The five-step Tame and Reframe strategy will not work for you if you are unable to properly use the Three E's and get educated on important topics. Disinformation is the new gold rush. **Spreading false information for internet clicks is making some companies rich while destroying public confidence.** Don't fall for it. Learn how to access and interpret information online.

Here are some important guidelines to help you:

- Journalism is a profession with standards and requirements. Not every source that pretends to be news is from a journalistic source. When interpreting news, take note of the following points from the American Press Institute, adapted from the book *The Elements of Journalism* by Bill Kovach and Tom Rosenstiel:
- Journalism must be truthful.
- Journalism's loyalty is to the citizens (not to bosses, advertisers, government, political leaders, or anyone else).
- Journalists verify their information in a variety of ways. This might mean interviewing multiple witnesses, disclosing sources, or asking more than one side for a comment on an issue. This is one key way that journalism is different from other means of communication like advertising, fiction, or opinion.
- Journalists must be independent from the news they cover.
- Journalists serve as watchdogs to monitor power and examine unseen areas of society.
- Journalism should represent a variety of viewpoints and find areas of common ground.
- Journalists should make important news interesting.
- Journalists should keep news truthful by also keeping it proportional. Certain news topics shouldn't be inflated and sensationalized while other news is underreported.
- Journalists should have a personal sense of ethics and the ability to voice their opinions and concerns within their organizations.
- Now that anyone with a smartphone can disseminate information, it's important for journalists to step in to clarify and fact-check information.[1]

- Refer to at least three reputable news sources. So no, you cannot rely on Facebook memes for your information. Look for public broadcasting, network news, overseas news, cable news, and respected publications. Compare and contrast multiple sources. Here are a few sources to consider: NPR, BBC, Democracy Now, Al Jazeera, and PBS.
- Apply your own reason and common sense. Use critical thinking skills. That means you shouldn't simply believe what you read or hear at face value. You must question it. Is it coming from an unbiased source? Is there money to be made from sensational information? Is it logical? How does it compare to other information sources and ideas? Finally, make a judgment about what you believe to be true.
- When in doubt, use respected fact-checking sites like Snopes.com, PolitiFact.com, and FactCheck.org.

In this new age of disinformation for profit, it's important to make the distinction between what is real and what isn't. Nobody can do that for you. Do your research for yourself and use your own critical thinking skills so you cannot be taken advantage of.

Recommended Resources

COACHING AND PERSONAL DEVELOPMENT

Resources

- BetterUp
  https://betterup.com
- International Coaching Federation
  https://coachingfederation.org
- Trish Ahjel Roberts
  https://trishahjelroberts.com

Books

Super Attractor by Gabby Bernstein
The Success Principles by Jack Canfield
Atomic Habits by James Clear
Change Your Habits, Change Your Life by Tom Corley
Becoming Supernatural by Dr Joe Dispenza
How to Solve Our Human Problems by Geshe Kelsang Gyatso
My Grandmother's Hands by Resmaa Menakem
Awaken the Giant Within by Tony Robbins
12 Steps to Mind-Blowing Happiness by Trish Ahjel Roberts
Thinking Outside the Chrysalis by Trish Ahjel Roberts
Happy for No Reason by Marci Shimoff

Podcasts

- Dear Gabby
  https://gabbybernstein.com/podcast
- Mind-Blowing Happiness Podcast
  https://trishahjelroberts.com/podcast

COMPASSION AND PLANT-BASED LIFESTYLE

Resources

- Apex Advocacy
  https://apexadvocacy.org
- Beyond Carnism
  https://carnism.org
- Follow Your Kind
  https://followyourkind.com
- Glue and Glitter Vegan Recipes
  https://glueandglitter.com
- The Humane League
  https://thehumaneleague.org
- Kadampa Meditation Centers
  https://kadampa.org/kadampa-meditation-centers
- The Kind Life
  https://thekindlife.com
- People for the Ethical Treatment of Animals
  https://peta.org
- Physician's Committee for Responsible Medicine
  https://pcrm.org
- Tabitha Brown
  https://iamtabithabrown.com

Books

Let Plants Nourish You by D. Natasha Brewley
Skinny Bitch by Rory Freedman
Veganize and Heal Your Life by Neeta Sanders

Films

Cowspiracy: The Sustainability Secret (2016)
Forks over Knives (2011)
The Game Changers (2019)
Vegucated (2011)
What the Health (2017)

ENTREPRENEURSHIP AND BUSINESS

Resources

- Happy Black Woman
  https://happyblackwoman.com
- Hello Seven
  https://helloseven.co
- Noomii Business Coaches
  https://noomii.com/business-coaches
- Patty Aubery Consulting
  https://pattyaubery.com

Podcasts

- Hello Seven
  https://helloseven.co/podcast-page
- The Social Proof
  https://thesocialproofpodcast.com

EDUCATION AND FACT CHECKING

Resources

- Coursera
  https://coursera.org
- EdX
  https://edx.org
- Fact Check
  https://factcheck.org

- Khan Academy
  https://khanacademy.org
- Politifact
  https://politifact.com
- Snopes
  https://snopes.com
- TedEd
  https://ed.ted.com
- Udemy
  https://udemy.com

EMPATHY AND DIVERSITY

Books

I Know Why the Caged Bird Sings by Maya Angelou
Self-Made by A'Lelia Bundles
The Alchemist by Paulo Coelho
Finding Me by Viola Davis
Homegoing by Yaa Gyasi
Autobiography of Malcolm X by Alex Haley
The Kite Runner by Khaled Hosseini
The Story of My Life by Helen Keller
I'm Glad My Mom Died by Jennette McCurdy
Thinking Outside the Chrysalis by Trish Ahjel Roberts
I Know Who You Are but What Am I? by Ali Sands
Autobiography of a Yogi by Paramhansa Yoganda
I Am Malala by Malala Yousafzai

Films

The African Doctor (2016)
Aloe Vera (2020)
Amélie (2001)
Like Cotton Twines (2017)
Like Water for Chocolate (1993)
The Platform (2019)
Train to Busan (2016)

MEDITATION AND MINDFULNESS

Resources

- Calm
https://calm.com
- Chopra
https://chopra.com/app
- Gabby Bernstein
https://gabbybernstein.com/freemeditations
- Gaia
https://gaia.com
- Headspace
https://headspace.com
- Insight Timer
https://insighttimer.com
- Joe Dispenza
https://drjoedispenza.com
- Kadampa Meditation Centers
https://kadampa.org/kadampa-meditation-centers

MENTAL HEALTH AND THERAPY

Resources

- Bad Bitches Have Bad Days Too
https://badbitcheshavebaddaystoo.com
- Better Help
https://betterhelp.com
- Mental Wealth Alliance
https://mentalwealthalliance.org
- Psychology Today
https://psychologytoday.com/us/therapists
- Therapy for Black Girls
https://therapyforblackgirls.com

SOCIAL JUSTICE

Resources

- Adrienne Maree Brown
  https://adriennemareebrown.net
- Grassroots Law
  https://grassrootslaw.org/team
- Ibram X. Kendi
  https://ibramxkendi.com
- NAACP
  https://naacp.org
- Resmaa Menakem
  https://resmaa.com
- Until Freedom
  https://untilfreedom.com

SOCIAL MEDIA AND ALGORITHMS

Films

The Social Dilemma (2020)
Stare into the Lights My Pretties (2017)

YOGA AND BREATHWORK

Resources

- Chitra Sukhu
  https://chitrasukhu.com
- Faith Hunter
  https://faithhunter.com
- Jaimee Ratliff
  https://jaimeeratliff.com

- MindBody
  https://mindbodyonline.com/explore
- My Vinyasa Practice
  https://myvinyasapractice.com
- Laughter Yoga
  https://www.laughteryoga.org

Acknowledgments

First and foremost, thank you to my literary agent, Gary Krebs, for believing in me and working tirelessly on my behalf. A huge thank you to Jack Canfield for sharing his vast wisdom with me and supporting my work with his powerful book foreword. Thank you to my editors, Debra Englander, Suzanne Staszak-Silva, and Crystal Branson for being patient as I slowly gave birth to this beautiful work. Much love and gratitude to my mentors and endorsers, Marci Shimoff and Patty Aubery. You two ladies exemplify what it means to support and empower women.

A big shout-out to all of my wonderful endorsers: Natasha Brewley, Paul Chen, Mayra Cuevas, Christopher Eubanks, Faith Hunter, Neeta Sanders, Serena Satcher, Chitra Sukhu, and Michelle Young. I am a deep believer that everything happens in life to fuel our growth and our paths have crossed for powerful reasons. Your friendship and support mean the world to me.

Thank you to my amazing Mind-Blowing Happiness™ Advisory Board, who have been on this journey with me since day one: Ebony Dixon, Jacqueline Fairley, Tamara Guillou, Catherine Johnson, and Tiffani Tucker.

Much love to my circle of besties who laugh, travel, and dance with me and cosign all my crazy ideas: Danté Dunham, Tami Guillou, Delores "Lucy" Rapoport, and Louis Roberts. There are no words for the support and love you show me.

Thank you to Jacqueline Flynn, Joanne Wattenberg, and the team at Rowman and Littlefield for teaching this newbie the ropes.

Thank you to Steve Harrison and the coaching team at Bradley Communications: Geoffrey Berwind, Sarah Brown, Valerie Costa, Laura Harrison, Mary Lou Reid, Cristina Smith, and Lynn Tramonte. Meeting and working with all of you is a joy and a privilege.

Thank you to my smart, creative sister-friend publicist, Carla Williams Johnson, for helping me get my message out into the world. You are amazing!

Thank you to my all-grown-up daughter Kayla for being my why. May you know a world where people can rise to their fullest potential and act in service to each other. Life is a journey. Don't ever stop growing, learning, and becoming the best person you can be.

Thank you to my strong, beautiful sister Chrissy and my handsome, talented nephew Carl for your love and encouragement. And thank you to the best dog and snuggle buddy in the world, my sweet Cooper.

We can create the world we want to live in. Let's do it. I love you all.

Notes

INTRODUCTION

1. M. Scott Peck, *The Road Less Traveled: A New Psychology of Love, Traditional Values, and Spiritual Growth* (New York: Simon and Schuster, 1978), 278.

CHAPTER 1

1. Merriam-Webster, "Anger," https://www.merriam-webster.com/dictionary/anger (accessed September 28, 2023).
2. Collins Dictionary, "Anger," https://www.collinsdictionary.com/dictionary/english/anger (accessed September 28, 2023).
3. Geshe Kelsang Gyatso, *How to Solve Our Human Problems: The Four Noble Truths* (London: Tharpa, 2007), pg. 21.

CHAPTER 2

1. American Heritage Dictionary, "Disappoint," October 6, 2023. https://www.ahdictionary.com/word/search.html?q=disappoint (accessed October 6, 2023).
2. American Heritage Dictionary, "Annoy," https://www.ahdictionary.com/word/search.html?q=annoy (accessed October 6, 2023).
3. Merriam-Webster, "Frustration," https://www.merriam-webster.com/dictionary/frustration (accessed October 7, 2023).

4. Merriam-Webster, "Jealous," https://www.merriam-webster.com/dictionary/jealous (accessed October 7, 2023).

5. Gabrielle Bernstein, *Super Attractor: Methods for Manifesting a Life beyond Your Wildest Dreams* (New York: Hay House, 2019).

6. Merriam-Webster, "Impatient," https://www.merriam-webster.com/dictionary/impatient (accessed October 7, 2023).

7. Merriam-Webster, "Guilt," https://www.merriam-webster.com/dictionary/guilt (accessed October 7, 2023).

8. Merriam-Webster, "Resentment," https://www.merriam-webster.com/dictionary/resentment (accessed October 7, 2023).

9. Merriam-Webster, "Create," https://www.merriam-webster.com/dictionary/create (accessed October 8, 2023).

10. Centers for Disease Control and Prevention, "State Specific Cost of Motor Vehicle Crash Deaths," November 5, 2020, https://www.cdc.gov/transportationsafety/statecosts/index.html.

11. Sarah Burd-Sharps, "Road Rage Shootings Are Continuing to Surge," Everytown Research, March 20, 2023, https://everytownresearch.org/reports-of-road-rage-shootings-are-on-the-rise/.

12. Dai Shirui et al., "Chronic Stress Promotes Cancer Development," *Frontiers in Oncology* 10 (2020), https://doi.org/10.3389/fonc.2020.01492.

CHAPTER 3

1. A. W. Siegman, "Cardiovascular Consequences of Expressing, Experiencing, and Repressing Anger," *Journal of Behavioral Medicine* 16, no. 6 (1993): 539–69, https://doi.org/10.1007/bf00844719.

CHAPTER 4

1. Moshe Ratson, "The Value of Anger: 16 Reasons It's Good to Get Angry," *Good Therapy* (blog), March 13, 2017, https://www.goodtherapy.org/blog/value-of-anger-16-reasons-its-good-to-get-angry-0313175.

2. "Bruce Lee Quotes," GoodReads, https://www.goodreads.com/author/quotes/32579.Bruce_Lee (accessed April 15, 2023).

3. Michael Patrick, "123 Knockout Mike Tyson Quotes about Discipline, Success, Money and More," *Parade*, February 26, 2023, https://parade.com/celebrities/mike-tyson-quotes.

4. "Lao Tzu Quotes," GoodReads, https://www.goodreads.com/author/quotes/2622245.Lao_Tzu (accessed April 15, 2023).

5. Kevin Bennett, "Rage Rooms Not a Good Idea," *Psychology Today*, March 30, 2017, https://www.psychologytoday.com/us/blog/modern-minds /201703/rage-rooms-not-good-idea.

6. Legal Dictionary, "Verbal Abuse," https://legaldictionary.net/verbal -abuse/ (accessed April 15, 2023).

7. National Institutes of Health, "Emotional Wellness Toolkit," updated August 8, 2022, https://www.nih.gov/health-information/emotional-wellness -toolkit.

8. M. Dittman, "Angry People Can Gain More in Certain Negotiations," *Monitor on Psychology* 35, no. 3 (March 2004), https://www.apa.org/monitor /mar04/angry.

9. Tasha Eurich, "What Self-Awareness Really Is and How to Cultivate It," *Harvard Business Review*, January 4, 2018, https://hbr.org/2018/01/what-self -awareness-really-is-and-how-to-cultivate-it.

CHAPTER 5

1. Reference.com, "How Many Times a Day Does the Average Human Breathe?," updated March 25, 2020,
https://www.reference.com/science-technology/many-times-average-human -breath-day-d3a07adf198e4794.

2. Jenna Fletcher, "How Long Can the Average Person Hold Their Breath?," *Medical News Today*, November 25, 2020, https://www.medicalnewstoday.com /articles/how-long-can-the-average-person-hold-their-breath.

3. Maamer Slamani, "Effects of Mental Imagery on Muscular Strength in Healthy and Patient Participants: A Systematic Review," *Journal of Sports Science and Medicine* 15, no. 3 (2016): 434–50, http://www.ncbi.nlm.nih.gov/pmc /articles/pmc4974856/.

4. Joe Dispenza, *Becoming Supernatural: How Common People Are Doing the Uncommon* (New York: Hay House, 2017).

CHAPTER 6

1. People for the Ethical Treatment of Animals, "Animals Used for Food," https://www.peta.org/issues/animals-used-for-food/ (accessed April 15).

2. *Environmental Health Perspectives*, "Environmental Racism Collection: Exposure and Health Inequities in Black Americans," updated July 31, 2020, https://ehp.niehs.nih.gov/curated-collections/environmental-racism.

CHAPTER 7

1. *Encyclopedia Britannica*, "Madam C.J. Walker," updated September 7, 2021, https://www.britannica.com/biography/Madam-C-J-Walker.

2. *Encyclopedia Britannica*, "Steve Jobs," updated July 30, 2021, https://www.britannica.com/biography/Steve-Jobs#ref280812.

3. *Encyclopedia Britannica*, "Steve Jobs."

4. *Encyclopedia Britannica*, "Sara Blakely," updated February 10, 2021, https://www.britannica.com/biography/Sara-Blakely.

5. Spanx Foundation, "About Us," https://www.spanxfoundation.com/about/ (accessed April 21, 2023).

6. United States Census Bureau, "Women Business Ownership in America on the Rise," March 24, 2021, https://www.census.gov/library/stories/2021/03/women-business-ownership-in-america-on-rise.html.

7. Elaine Pofeldt, "How More Women Can Break the $1 Million Mark," *Forbes*, September 28, 2018, https://www.forbes.com/sites/elainepofeldt/2018/09/28/how-more-women-can-break-the-1-million-mark/?sh=2e01ffb7df19.

8. Matthew Speiser, "Women-Owned Business Statistics: A Guide to Women Entrepreneurs," Fundera, updated January 23, 2023, https://www.fundera.com/resources/women-owned-business-statistics.

9. Spanx Foundation, "About Us."

10. Helen Rosner, "How Slutty Vegan Puts the Party in Plant-Based Food," *New Yorker*, April 17, 2023, https://www.newyorker.com/magazine/2023/04/17/how-slutty-vegan-puts-the-party-in-plant-based-food.

11. Micah Solomon, "The Slutty Vegan Founder Pinky Cole on Her Wild Success Bringing Playful Vegan Food to the Fore," *Forbes*, July 12, 2019, https://www.forbes.com/sites/micahsolomon/2019/07/12/the-slutty-vegan-founder-pinky-cole-on-her-wild-success-bringing-playful-vegan-food-to-the-fore/.

12. Pinky Cole, *Eats Plants, B*tch: 91 Vegan Recipes That Will Blow Your Meat-Loving Mind* (New York: Penguin Random House, 2021).

13. Slutty Vegan, "About," https://sluttyveganatl.com/about/ (accessed April 21, 2023).

14. Cole, *Eats Plants, B*tch.*

15. Sarah McLaughlin, "Slutty Vegan Brings Its Plant-Based Burgers to NYC This Month," *Green Matters*, September 8, 2021, https://www.greenmatters.com/food/slutty-vegan-nyc.

16. Kadia Tubman, "A Look at Black-Owned Businesses in the U.S.," Pew Research Center, February 21, 2023, https://www.pewresearch.org/fact-tank/2023/02/21/a-look-at-black-owned-businesses-in-the-u-s/.

17. Hello Seven, "About," https://helloseven.co/about/ (accessed April 21, 2023).

18. Rachel Rodgers, *We Should All Be Millionaires: A Woman's Guide to Earning More, Building Wealth, and Gaining Economic Power* (New York: HarperCollins Leadership, 2021).

19. Lydia Dishman, "Counselor: How Rachel Rodgers Built Her Virtual Legal Practice," *Fast Company*, April 15, 2013, https://www.fastcompany.com /3008304/counselor-how-rachel-rodgers-built-her-virtual-legal-practice.

CHAPTER 8

1. Mark Stibich, "Top Reasons to Smile Every Day," Verywell Mind, updated February 17, 2023, https://www.verywellmind.com/top-reasons-to -smile-every-day-2223755.

2. Mayo Clinic, "Massage Therapy," https://www.mayoclinic.org/tests -procedures/massage-therapy/about/pac-20384595 (accessed April 25, 2023).

3. Harvard Medical School, "Saunas and Your Health," Harvard Health Publishing, https://www.health.harvard.edu/staying-healthy/saunas-and-your -health (accessed April 25, 2023).

4. Stephanie Watson, "What Are the Benefits of Infrared Saunas?," Healthline, Healthline Media, September 26, 2019, https://www.healthline.com/health /infrared-sauna-benefits#What-is-an-infrared-sauna.

5. BetterHelp, "What Is Animal Therapy?," https://www.betterhelp.com/ advice/therapy/what-is-animal-therapy/ (accessed April 25, 2023).

6. Laughter Yoga International, "About Laughter Yoga," https://www .laughteryoga.org/about-laughter-yoga/ (accessed April 25, 2023).

7. Merriam-Webster, "Self-Validation," https://www.merriam-webster.com/ dictionary/self-validation (accessed October 11, 2023).

8. Cambridge Dictionary, "Self-Affirmation," https://dictionary.cambridge .org/dictionary/english/self-affirmation (accessed October 11, 2023).

9. Kendra Cherry, "Positive Reinforcement in Psychology: Definition + 5 Examples," Simply Psychology, https://www.simplypsychology.org/positive -reinforcement.html (accessed April 25, 2023).

10. James Clear, "The Ultimate Guide to Building Habits That Stick," JamesClear.com, https://jamesclear.com/habit-guide (accessed April 25, 2023).

11. James Clear, *Atomic Habits: An Easy & Proven Way to Build Good Habits & Break Bad Ones* (New York: Avery, 2018).

CHAPTER 9

1. Merriam-Webster, "Happiness," https://www.merriam-webster.com/dictionary/happiness (accessed October 11, 2023).

2. Philip Kanske, "Dissecting the Social Brain: Introducing the EmpaToM to Reveal Distinct Neural Networks and Brain–Behavior Relations for Empathy and Theory of Mind," *NeuroImage* 122 (November 2015): 6–19. https://doi.org/10.1016/j.neuroimage.2015.07.082.

3. Jennifer Mascia and Chip Brownlee, "A Decade of Mass Shootings by the Numbers," The Trace, October 5, 2023, https://www.thetrace.org/2023/10/mass-shootings-gun-violence-how-many/.

4. Saul McLeod, "Maslow's Hierarchy of Needs," Simple Psychology, updated October 2, 2023, https://www.simplypsychology.org/maslow.html

5. Olivia Munson, "What Is an Empath? Expert Explains the Personality Type and How to Know If You Are One," *USA Today*, April 12, 2023, https://www.usatoday.com/story/life/health-wellness/2022/11/02/what-is-an-empath/8083279001/.

6. *Psychology Today*, "Codependency," https://www.psychologytoday.com/us/basics/codependency (accessed April 15, 2023).

7. Lois Zoppi, "What Is Trauma Bonding?," *Medical News Today*, November 27, 2020, https://www.medicalnewstoday.com/articles/trauma-bonding.

8. Marci Shimoff, *Happy for No Reason: 7 Steps to Being Happy from the Inside Out* (New York: Free Press, 2008).

9. Trish Ahjel Roberts, *12 Steps to Mind-Blowing Happiness: A Journal of Insights, Quotes, & Questions to Juice Up Your Journey* (Atlanta: Mind-Blowing Happiness LLC, 2021), xiii.

10. IMDB, "Tootsie," https://www.imdb.com/title/tt0084805/characters/nm0000414 (accessed October 11, 2023).

11. Jack Canfield, *The Success Principles: How to Get from Where You Are to Where You Want to Be* (New York: William Morrow, 2005), 3.

12. Joe Dispenza, "Synchronizing Your Energy to New Potentials," *Unlimited/Dr. Joe Dispenza* (blog), October 9, 2020, https://drjoedispenza.com/blogs/dr-joes-blog/synchronizing-your-energy-to-new-potentials.

13. Physicians Committee for Responsible Medicine, "Plant-Based Nutrition FAQ," https://www.pcrm.org/good-nutrition/plant-based-diets/nutrition-faq (accessed April 15, 2023).

14. World Atlas, "Countries by Percentage of World Population," https://www.worldatlas.com/articles/countries-by-percentage-of-world-population.html (accessed April 15, 2023).

15. Ranker, "53 Celebrities Who Have Been Homeless," https://www.ranker.com/list/famous-people-who-were-homeless/celebrity-lists (accessed October 11, 2023).

16. People for the Ethical Treatment of Animals, "Why Animal Rights?" https://www.peta.org/about-peta/why-peta/why-animal-rights/ (accessed April 15, 2023).

17. Our World in Data, "Yearly Number of Animals Slaughtered for Meat: World 1961–2021," https://ourworldindata.org/grapher/animals -slaughtered-for-meat (accessed April 15, 2023).

18. Kelly Anthis, "Global Farmed and Factory Farmed Animals Estimates," Sentience Institute, updated February 21, 2019, https://www.sentienceinstitute .org/global-animal-farming-estimates.

19. World Health Organization, "Stop Using Antibiotics in Healthy Animals to Prevent the Spread of Antibiotic Resistance," November 7, 2017, https:// www.who.int/news/item/07-11-2017-stop-using-antibiotics-in-healthy-animals -to-prevent-the-spread-of-antibiotic-resistance.

20. Centers for Disease Control and Prevention, "More People in the United States Dying from Antibiotic-Resistant Infections than Previously Estimated," November 13, 2019, https://www.cdc.gov/media/releases/2019/p1113 -antibiotic-resistant.html.

21. Betsy Reed, "Millions of US Farm Animals to be Culled by Suffocation, Drowning and Shooting," *Guardian*, May 29, 2020, https://www.theguardian .com/environment/2020/may/19/millions-of-us-farm-animals-to-be-culled-by -suffocation-drowning-and-shooting-coronavirus.

CHAPTER 10

1. Free Dictionary, "Venting," https://www.thefreedictionary.com/venting (accessed April 28, 2023).

2. Thought Hub, "The Psychology of Venting," Southwestern Assemblies of God University, https://www.sagu.edu/thoughthub/the-psychology-of -venting/ (accessed April 28, 2023).

3. Coursera, "Active Listening," updated September 28, 2017, https://www .coursera.org/articles/active-listening.

4. Rhonda Byrne, *The Secret* (New York: Atria Books/Beyond Words, 2006).

5. Joe Dispenza, *Tuning in to New Potentials* (New York: Hay House, 2013).

6. Emily Green, "The Benefits of Meditation: 80 Reasons to Practice Mindfulness," Positive Psychology, updated March 9, 2022, https://positivepsychology .com/benefits-of-meditation/.

7. Roko Belic, dir., *Happy* (Wadi Rum Productions, 2011); Louie Psihoyos, *The Game Changers* (Game Changers Film LLC, 2019).

CHAPTER 11

1. Anthony Robbins, *Awaken the Giant Within: How to Take Immediate Control of Your Mental, Emotional, Physical and Financial Destiny!* (New York: Simon and Schuster, 1991), 25.

2. Tom Corley, *Change Your Habits, Change Your Life: Strategies that Transformed 177 Average People into Self-Made Millionaires* (Dallas: Ben-Bella Books, 2016), 45.

3. Jim Collins and Jerry Porras, *Built to Last: Successful Habits of Visionary Companies* (New York: HarperCollins, 1994), 56.

4. Ron Elving, "Norman Vincent Peale Was a Conservative Hero, Known Well Beyond His Era," NPR, July 24, 2020, https://www.npr.org/2020/07/24/894967922/norman-vincent-peale-was-a-conservative-hero-known-well-beyond-his-era.

5. Steve Scott, "Big Hairy Audacious Goals: Definition, Tips and Examples," Develop Good Habits, https://www.developgoodhabits.com/big-hairy-audacious-goals/ (accessed April 28, 2023).

APPENDIX

1. American Press Institute, "The Elements of Journalism," https://www.americanpressinstitute.org/journalism-essentials/what-is-journalism/elements-journalism/.

Bibliography

AAA. "Aggressive Driving." AAA Exchange. https://exchange.aaa.com/safety /driving-advice/aggressive-driving/ (accessed April 15, 2023).

Alfonseca, Kiara. "There Have Been More Mass Shootings Than Days in 2023, Database Shows." ABC News, April 10, 2023. https://abcnews.go.com/US/ mass-shootings-days-2023-database-shows/story?id=96609874.

American Press Institute. "The Elements of Journalism." https://www .americanpressinstitute.org/journalism-essentials/what-is-journalism/ elements-journalism/.

Anthis, Kelly. "Global Farmed and Factory Farmed Animals Estimates." Sentience Institute, updated February 21, 2019. https://www.sentienceinstitute .org/global-animal-farming-estimates.

Belic, Roko, dir. *Happy*. Wadi Rum Productions, 2011.

Bennett, Kevin. "Rage Rooms Not a Good Idea." *Psychology Today*, March 30, 2017. https://www.psychologytoday.com/us/blog/modern-minds/201703 /rage-rooms-not-good-idea.

Bernstein, Gabrielle. *Super Attractor: Methods for Manifesting a Life beyond Your Wildest Dreams*. New York: Hay House, 2019.

BetterHelp. "What Is Animal Therapy?" https://www.betterhelp.com/advice/ therapy/what-is-animal-therapy/ (accessed April 25, 2023).

Brown, Brené. *Daring Greatly: How the Courage to Be Vulnerable Transforms the Way We Live, Love, Parent, and Lead*. New York: Gotham Books, 2012.

Burd-Sharps, Sarah. "Road Rage Shootings Are Continuing to Surge." Everytown Research, March 20, 2023. https://everytownresearch.org/reports -of-road-rage-shootings-are-on-the-rise/.

Byrne, Rhonda. *The Secret*. New York: Atria Books/Beyond Words, 2006.

Canfield, Jack. *The Success Principles: How to Get from Where You Are to Where You Want to Be*. New York: William Morrow, 2005.

Centers for Disease Control and Prevention. "More People in the United States Dying from Antibiotic-Resistant Infections than Previously Estimated."

November 13, 2019. https://www.cdc.gov/media/releases/2019/p1113
-antibiotic-resistant.html.

———. "State Specific Cost of Motor Vehicle Crash Deaths." November 5,
2020. https://www.cdc.gov/transportationsafety/statecosts/index.html.

Cherry, Kendra. "Positive Reinforcement in Psychology: Definition +
5 Examples." Simply Psychology. https://www.simplypsychology.org/
positive-reinforcement.html (accessed April 25, 2023).

Clear, James. *Atomic Habits: An Easy & Proven Way to Build Good Habits &
Break Bad Ones*. New York: Avery, 2018.

———. "The Ultimate Guide to Building Habits That Stick." JamesClear.com.
https://jamesclear.com/habit-guide (accessed April 25, 2023).

Cole, Pinky. *Eat Plants, B*tch: 91 Vegan Recipes That Will Blow Your
Meat-Loving Mind*. New York: Penguin Random House, 2021.

Collins, Jim, and Porras, Jerry. *Built to Last: Successful Habits of Visionary
Companies*. New York: HarperCollins, 1994.

Corley, Tom. *Change Your Habits, Change Your Life: Strategies that Transformed
177 Average People into Self-Made Millionaires*. Dallas: BenBella
Books, 2016.

Coursera. "Active Listening." Updated September 28, 2017. https://www
.coursera.org/articles/active-listening.

Dishman, Lydia. "Counselor: How Rachel Rodgers Built Her Virtual Legal
Practice." *Fast Company*, April 15, 2013. https://www.fastcompany.com
/3008304/counselor-how-rachel-rodgers-built-her-virtual-legal-practice.

Dispenza, Joe. *Becoming Supernatural: How Common People Are Doing the
Uncommon*. New York: Hay House, 2017.

———. "Synchronizing Your Energy to New Potentials." *Unlimited/Dr. Joe
Dispenza* (blog), October 9, 2020. https://drjoedispenza.com/blogs/dr-joes
-blog/synchronizing-your-energy-to-new-potentials.

———. *Tuning in to New Potentials*. New York: Hay House, 2013.

Dittman, M. "Angry People Can Gain More in Certain Negotiations." *Monitor
on Psychology* 35, no. 3 (March 2004). https://www.apa.org/monitor/mar04
/angry.

Economic Times. "Trip to India as Teen Was a Life Changer for Steve Jobs."
September 30, 2011, updated October 7, 2011. https://economictimes
.indiatimes.com/news/international/trip-to-india-as-teen-was-a-life-changer
-for-steve-jobs/articleshow/10264889.cms.

Elving, Ron. "Norman Vincent Peale Was a Conservative Hero, Known
Well Beyond His Era." NPR, July 24, 2020. https://www.npr.org/2020/07
/24/894967922/norman-vincent-peale-was-a-conservative-hero-known-well
-beyond-his-era.

Encyclopedia Britannica. "Madam C. J. Walker." Updated September 7,
2021. https://www.britannica.com/biography/Madam-C-J-Walker.

————. "Sara Blakely." Updated February 10, 2021. https://www.britannica.com/biography/Sara-Blakely.

————. "Steve Jobs." Updated July 30, 2021. https://www.britannica.com/biography/Steve-Jobs.

Environmental Health Perspectives. "Environmental Racism Collection: Exposure and Health Inequities in Black Americans." Updated July 31, 2020. https://ehp.niehs.nih.gov/curated-collections/environmental-racism.

Eurich, Tasha. "What Self-Awareness Really Is and How to Cultivate It." *Harvard Business Review*, January 4, 2018. https://hbr.org/2018/01/what-self-awareness-really-is-and-how-to-cultivate-it.

Fletcher, Jenna. "How Long Can the Average Person Hold Their Breath?" *Medical News Today*, November 25, 2020. https://www.medicalnewstoday.com/articles/how-long-can-the-average-person-hold-their-breath.

Frothingham, Mia Belle. "Emotional Intelligence (EQ): Definition, Components & Examples." Simply Psychology, updated March 29, 2023. https://www.simplypsychology.org/emotional-intelligence.html.

Green, Emily. "The Benefits of Meditation: 80 Reasons to Practice Mindfulness." Positive Psychology, updated March 9, 2022. https://positivepsychology.com/benefits-of-meditation/ (accessed April 28, 2023).

Gyatso, Geshe Kelsang. *How to Solve Our Human Problems: The Four Noble Truths*. London: Tharpa Publications, 2005.

Harvard Medical School. "Saunas and Your Health." Harvard Health Publishing. https://www.health.harvard.edu/staying-healthy/saunas-and-your-health (accessed April 25, 2023).

Hayes, Adam. "Bernie Madoff: Who He Was, How His Ponzi Scheme Worked." *Investopedia*, updated March 29, 2023. https://www.investopedia.com/terms/b/bernard-madoff.asp.

Hello Seven. "About." https://helloseven.co/about/ (accessed April 21, 2023).

Hernandez, Joe. "A Nun Stole $835,000 from a School to Feed a Gambling Habit, Prosecutors Say." NPR, June 10, 2021. https://www.npr.org/2021/06/10/1005101141/a-nun-stole-835-000-from-a-school-to-feed-a-gambling-habit-prosecutors-say.

Kanske, Philip. "Dissecting the Social Brain: Introducing the EmpaToM to Reveal Distinct Neural Networks and Brain-Behavior Relations for Empathy and Theory of Mind." *NeuroImage* 122 (November 2015): 6–19. https://doi.org/10.1016/j.neuroimage.2015.07.082.

Kubler-Ross, Elisabeth. *On Death and Dying: What the Dying Have to Teach Doctors, Nurses, Clergy, and Their Own Families*. New York: Simon and Schuster, 1969.

Laughter Yoga International. "About Laughter Yoga." https://www.laughteryoga.org/about-laughter-yoga/ (accessed April 25, 2023).

Mascia, Jennifer, and Chip Brownlee. "A Decade of Mass Shootings by the Numbers." The Trace, October 5, 2023. https://www.thetrace.org/2023/10/mass-shootings-gun-violence-how-many/.

McLeod, Saul. "Maslow's Hierarchy of Needs." Simple Psychology, updated October 2, 2023. https://www.simplypsychology.org/maslow.html.

National Institutes of Health. "Emotional Wellness Toolkit." Updated August 8, 2022. https://www.nih.gov/health-information/emotional-wellness-toolkit.

Mayo Clinic. "Massage Therapy." https://www.mayoclinic.org/tests-procedures/massage-therapy/about/pac-20384595 (accessed April 25, 2023).

McLaughlin, Sarah. "Slutty Vegan Brings Its Plant-Based Burgers to NYC This Month." *Green Matters*, September 8, 2021. https://www.greenmatters.com/food/slutty-vegan-nyc.

Minassian, Liana. "Why the Global Rise in Vegan and Plant-Based Eating Is No Fad." Food Revolution Network, April 6, 2022, updated April 10, 2023. https://foodrevolution.org/blog/vegan-statistics-global/.

Munson, Olivia. "What Is an Empath? Expert Explains the Personality Type and How to Know If You Are One." *USA Today*, April 12, 2023. https://www.usatoday.com/story/life/health-wellness/2022/11/02/what-is-an-empath/8083279001/.

Our World in Data. "Yearly Number of Animals Slaughtered for Meat: World 1961–2021." https://ourworldindata.org/grapher/animals-slaughtered-for-meat (accessed April 15, 2023).

Peck, M. Scott. *The Road Less Traveled: A New Psychology of Love, Traditional Values, and Spiritual Growth.* New York: Simon and Schuster, 1978.

People for the Ethical Treatment of Animals. "Animals Used for Food." https://www.peta.org/issues/animals-used-for-food/ (accessed April 15, 2023).

———. "Why Animal Rights?" https://www.peta.org/about-peta/why-peta/why-animal-rights/ (accessed April 15, 2023).

Physicians Committee for Responsible Medicine. "Plant-Based Nutrition FAQ." https://www.pcrm.org/good-nutrition/plant-based-diets/nutrition-faq (accessed April 15, 2023).

Plamondon, Andréanne. "Family Dynamics and Young Adults' Well-Being: The Mediating Role of Sibling Bullying." *Journal of Interpersonal Violence* 36, no. 9–10 (2021). https://doi.org/10.1177/0886260518800313.

Pofeldt, Elaine. "How More Women Can Break the $1 Million Mark." *Forbes*, September 28, 2018. https://www.forbes.com/sites/elainepofeldt/2018/09/28/how-more-women-can-break-the-1-million-mark/.

Psihoyos, Louie, dir. *The Game Changers.* Game Changers Film LLC, 2019.

Ratson, Moshe. "The Value of Anger: 16 Reasons It's Good to Get Angry." *Good Therapy* (blog), March 13, 2017. https://www.goodtherapy.org/blog/value-of-anger-16-reasons-its-good-to-get-angry-0313175.

Reed, Betsy. "Millions of US Farm Animals to Be Culled by Suffocation, Drowning and Shooting." *Guardian*, May 29, 2020. https://www.theguardian .com/environment/2020/may/19/millions-of-us-farm-animals-to-be-culled -by-suffocation-drowning-and-shooting-coronavirus.

Reference.com. "How Many Times a Day Does the Average Human Breathe?" Updated March 25, 2020. https://www.reference.com/science-technology/ many-times-average-human-breath-day-d3a07adf198e4794.

Roberts, Trish Ahjel. *12 Steps to Mind-Blowing Happiness: A Journal of Insights, Quotes, & Questions to Juice Up Your Journey.* Atlanta: Mind-Blowing Happiness LLC, 2021.

Robbins, Anthony. *Awaken the Giant Within: How to Take Immediate Control of Your Mental, Emotional, Physical and Financial Destiny!* New York: Simon and Schuster, 1991.

Rodgers, Rachel. *We Should All Be Millionaires: A Woman's Guide to Earning More, Building Wealth, and Gaining Economic Power.* New York: HarperCollins Leadership, 2021.

Rosner, Helen. "How Slutty Vegan Puts the Party in Plant-Based Food." *New Yorker*, April 17, 2023. https://www.newyorker.com/magazine/2023/04/17/ how-slutty-vegan-puts-the-party-in-plant-based-food.

Scott, Steve. "Big Hairy Audacious Goals: Definition, Tips and Examples." Develop Good Habits. https://www.developgoodhabits.com/big-hairy -audacious-goals (accessed April 28, 2023).

Shimoff, Marci. *Happy for No Reason: 7 Steps to Being Happy from the Inside Out.* New York: Atria, 2008.

Shiuri, Dai, et al. "Chronic Stress Promotes Cancer Development." *Frontiers in Oncology* 10 (2020). https://doi.org/10.3389/fonc.2020.01492.

Siegman, A. W. "Cardiovascular Consequences of Expressing, Experiencing, and Repressing Anger." *Journal of Behavioral Medicine* 16, no. 6 (1993): 539–69. https://doi.org/10.1007/bf00844719.

Slamani, Maamer. "Effects of Mental Imagery on Muscular Strength in Healthy and Patient Participants: A Systematic Review." *Journal of Sports Science and Medicine* 15, no. 3 (2016): 434–50. http://www.ncbi.nlm.nih.gov/pmc/ articles/pmc4974856/.

Slutty Vegan. "About." https://sluttyveganatl.com/about/ (accessed April 21, 2023).

Solomon, Micah. "The Slutty Vegan Founder Pinky Cole on Her Wild Success Bringing Playful Vegan Food to the Fore." *Forbes*, July 12, 2019. https:// www.forbes.com/sites/micahsolomon/2019/07/12/the-slutty-vegan-founder -pinky-cole-on-her-wild-success-bringing-playful-vegan-food-to-the-fore/.

Spanx Foundation. "About Us." https://www.spanxfoundation.com/about/ (accessed April 21, 2023).

Speiser, Matthew. "Women-Owned Business Statistics: A Guide to Women Entrepreneurs." Fundera, updated January 23, 2023. https://www.fundera .com/resources/women-owned-business-statistics.

Stibich, Mark. "Top Reasons to Smile Every Day." Verywell Mind, updated February 17, 2023. https://www.verywellmind.com/top-reasons-to-smile -every-day-2223755.

Thought Hub. "The Psychology of Venting." Southwestern Assemblies of God University. https://www.sagu.edu/thoughthub/the-psychology-of-venting/ (accessed April 28, 2023).

Tolley, Alejandra. "Plant-Based Meals Are Now the Default at New York City Hospitals." *VegOut*, October 4, 2022. https://vegoutmag.com/news/plant -based-hospitals/.

Tubman, Kadia. "A Look at Black-Owned Businesses in the U.S." Pew Research Center, February 21, 2023. https://www.pewresearch.org/fact-tank /2023/02/21/a-look-at-black-owned-businesses-in-the-u-s/.

United States Census Bureau. "Women Business Ownership in America on the Rise." March 24, 2021. https://www.census.gov/library/stories/2021/03/ women-business-ownership-in-america-on-rise.html.

Watson, Stephanie. "What Are the Benefits of Infrared Saunas?" Healthline, Healthline Media, September 26, 2019. https://www.healthline.com/health/ infrared-sauna-benefits#What-is-an-infrared-sauna

World Atlas. "Countries by Percentage of World Population." https://www .worldatlas.com/articles/countries-by-percentage-of-world-population.html (accessed April 15, 2023).

World Health Organization. "Stop Using Antibiotics in Healthy Animals to Prevent the Spread of Antibiotic Resistance." November 7, 2017. https: //www.who.int/news/item/07-11-2017-stop-using-antibiotics-in-healthy -animals-to-prevent-the-spread-of-antibiotic-resistance.

Zoppi, Lois. "What Is Trauma Bonding?" *Medical News Today*, November 27, 2020. https://www.medicalnewstoday.com/articles/trauma-bonding.

Index

About Trish Ahjel Roberts

Trish Ahjel Roberts is a transformational coach, inspirational speaker, and soul-healing retreat leader. She is the founder of the Mind-Blowing Happiness coaching company and the Black Vegan Life event brand. She is the author of the acclaimed self-help memoir *Thinking Outside the Chrysalis: A Black Woman's Guide to Spreading Her Wings* and the Amazon bestseller *12 Steps to Mind-Blowing Happiness*, which was endorsed by Jack Canfield, Marci Shimoff, and Iyanla Vanzant. In these books, she teaches her proprietary twelve-step path to a life of deep joy and fulfillment. She is a certified life coach, registered yoga and meditation instructor, and reiki practitioner with more than a decade of Buddhist study. She has been featured on CBS46-TV in Atlanta, WBLS-FM New York, and many other media platforms. She also hosts the Mind-Blowing Happiness Podcast. Trish was born and raised in Brooklyn, New York, and currently spends her time between Atlanta, Georgia, and Tampa, Florida. When she's not coaching, writing, speaking, or leading retreats, you can find her on the hiking trail, at the beach, in the yoga studio or curled up on the sofa with her dog Cooper. To find out more about Trish's keynote presentations, workshops, coaching packages, and books, you can contact her at:

Mind-Blowing Happiness LLC
235 Peachtree Street NE, Suite 400
Atlanta, GA 30303
Phone: 404-981-8889
Email: info@TrishAhjelRoberts.com
TrishAhjelRoberts.com / Follow @TrishAhjelRoberts on social media

Want to Experience Mind-Blowing Happiness?

Join the Academy

Are you ready to continue the journey to true self-love and get the support you need—mind, body, and spirit? The Mind-Blowing Happiness Academy is an online community for women, men, and nonbinary people of all backgrounds who want to reduce negative emotions, identify their superpowers, create new habits, and live a life of balance, joy, and purpose. No matter what is getting in the way of you living your most peaceful and deeply fulfilling life—whether it's lack of supportive community, shaky confidence, old habits, or just lack of information—The Mind-Blowing Happiness Academy has what you need. It's the perfect next step after reading this book.

We can help you create the life you *really* want.
- Get weekly guidance, make friends, and build community.
- Receive live coaching directly from Trish Ahjel Roberts and guest experts.
- Access all the resources and encouragement you need to slay self-doubt, limiting beliefs, and any other mental habits that steal your joy.

Join the Mind-Blowing Happiness Academy and take the next step on the journey to your best life ever.

Visit MindBlowingHappiness.com to learn more.